THIS COLORING BOOK BELONGS TO:

_____

Copyright © 2020 By Malika O'Neill

All rights reserved. No part of this book may be reproduced in any form on by an electronic or mechanical means, including information storage and retrieval systems, without permission in writing from the publisher, except by a reviewer who may quote brief passages in a review.

www.thepleasurecollectivellc.com

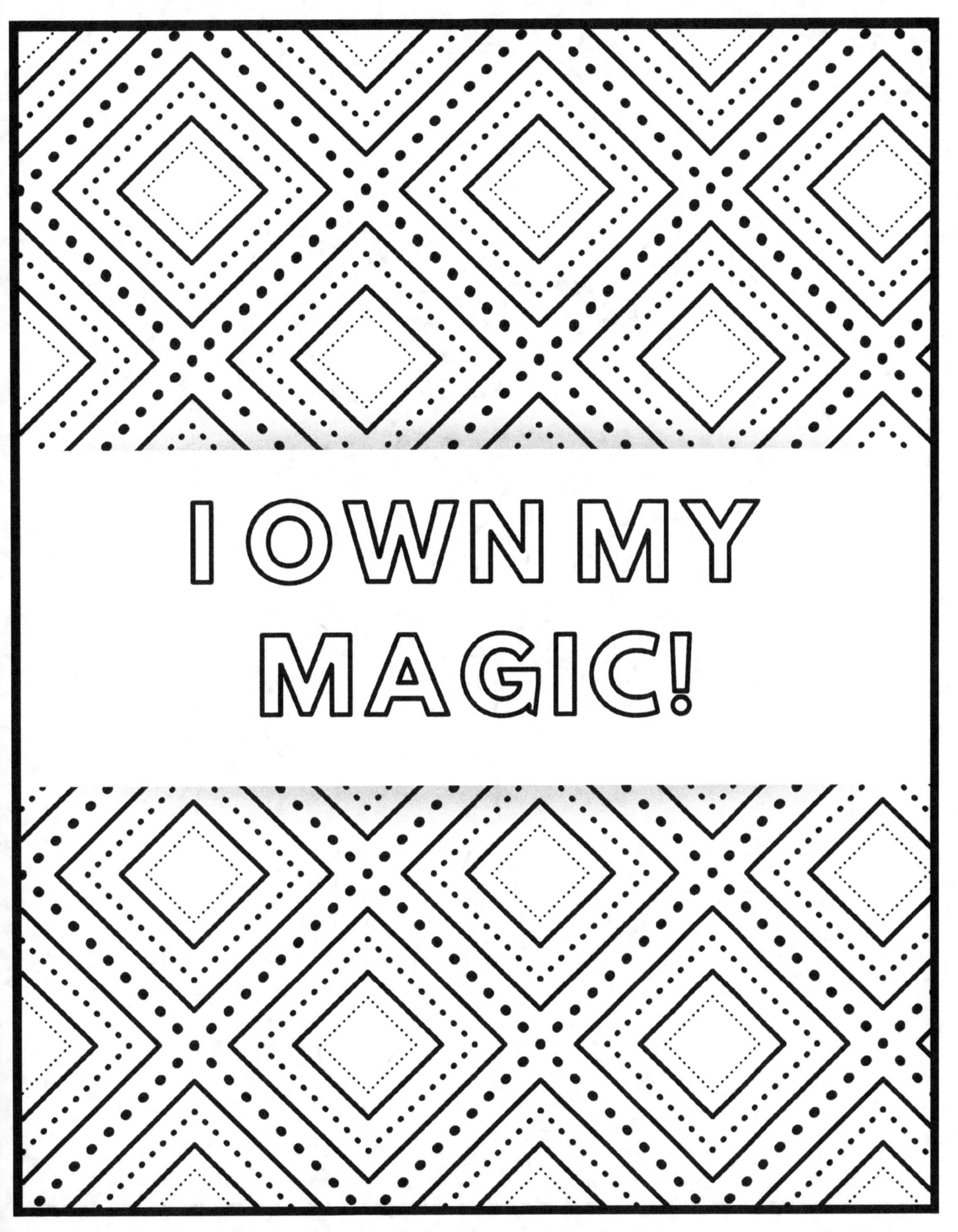

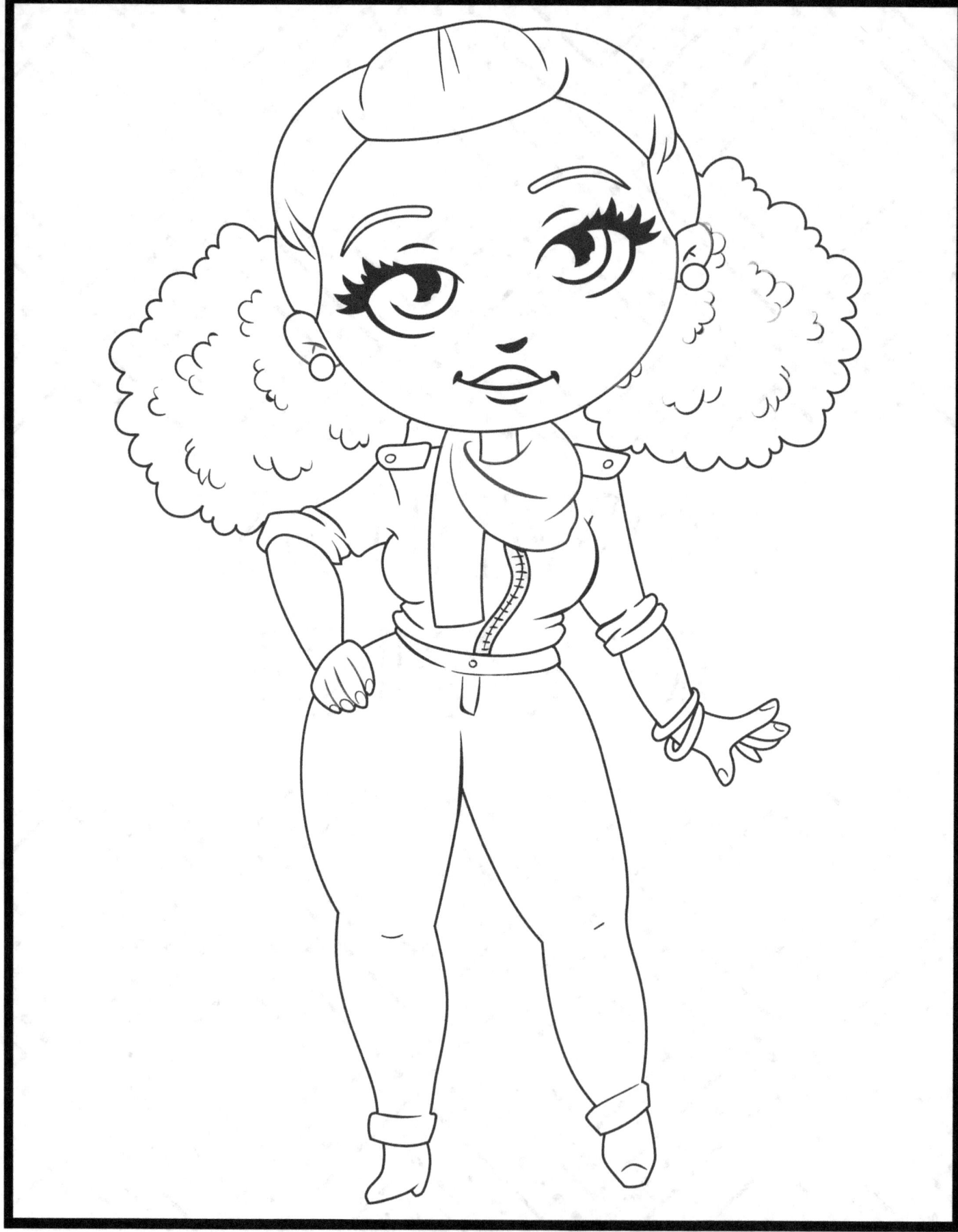

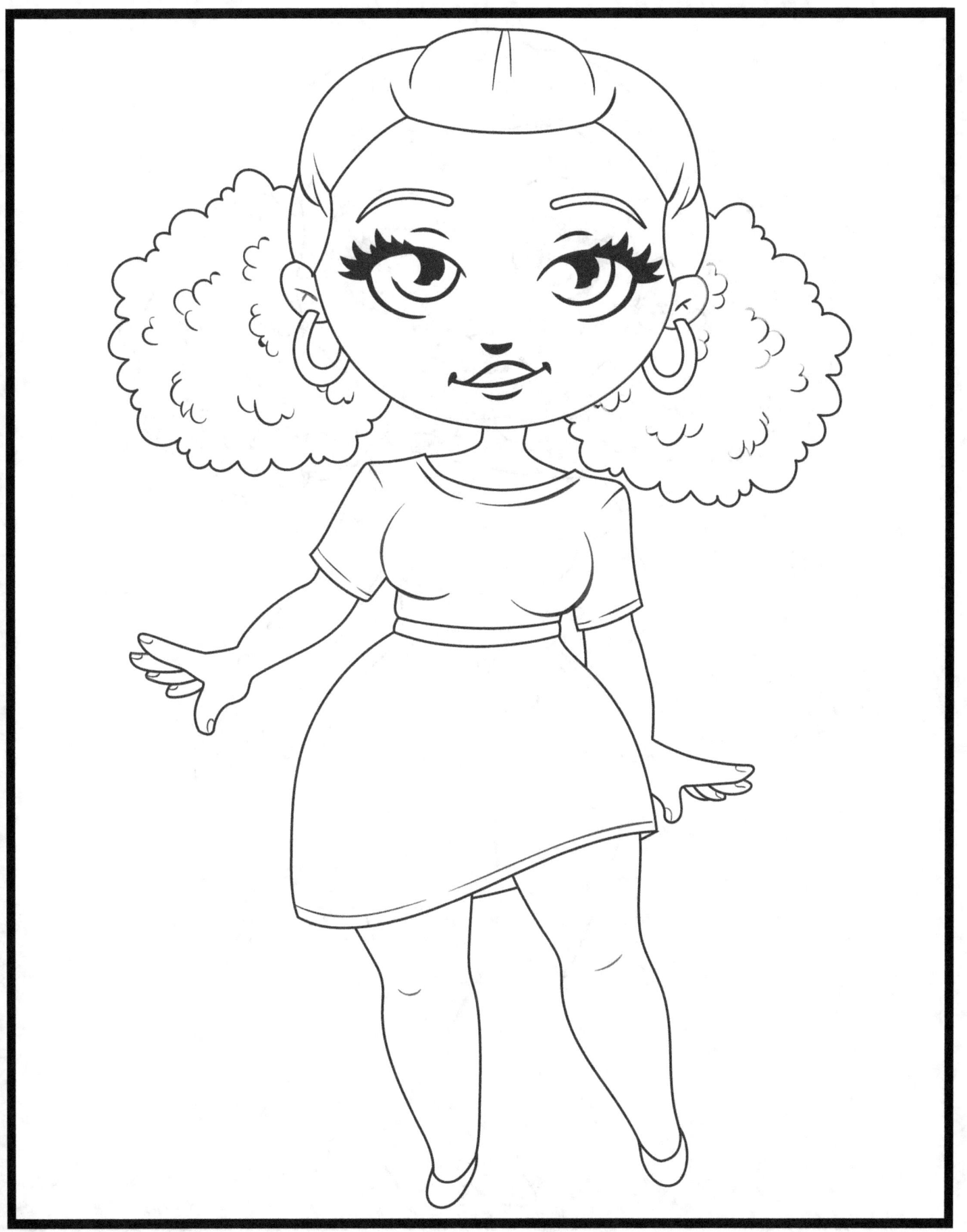

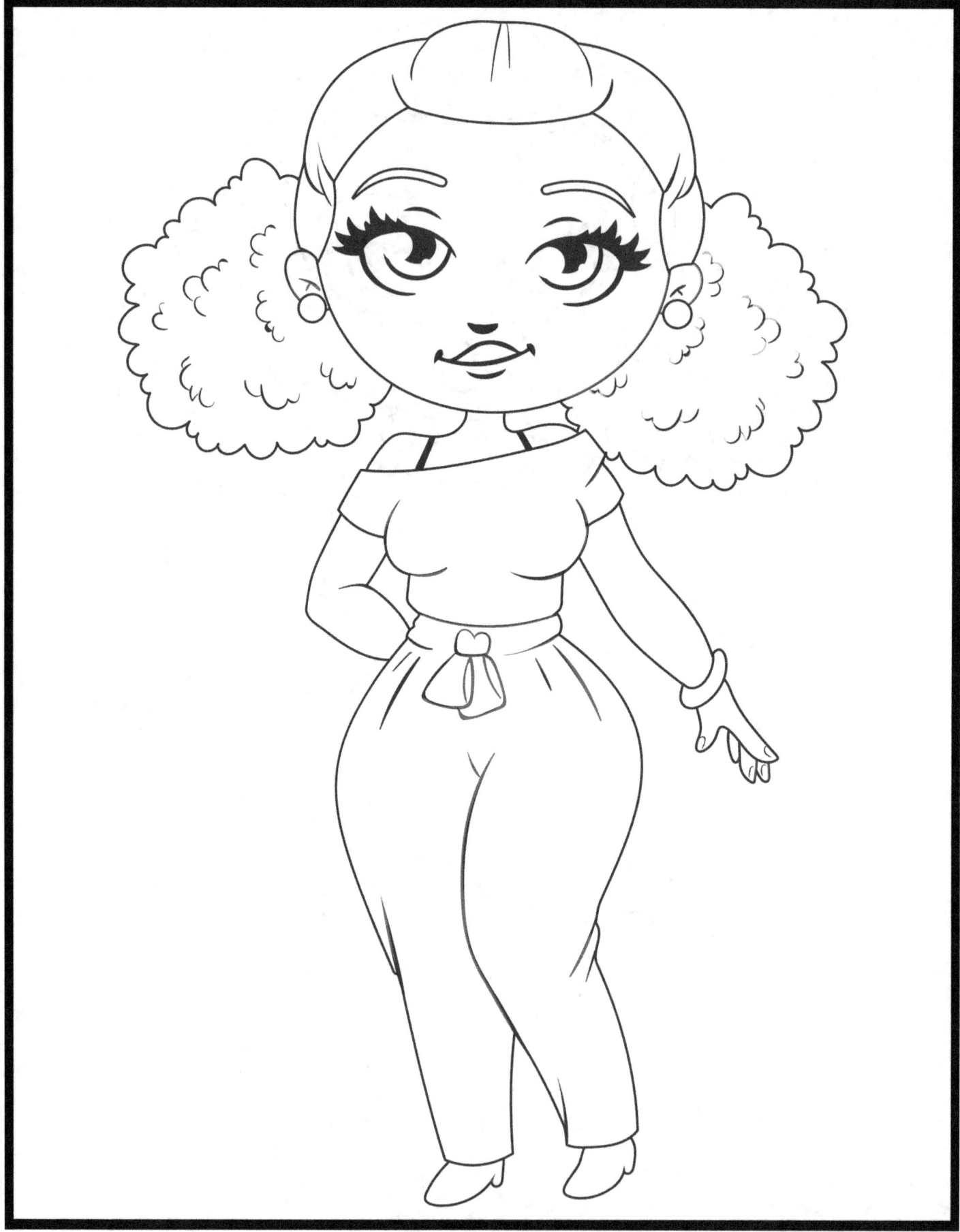

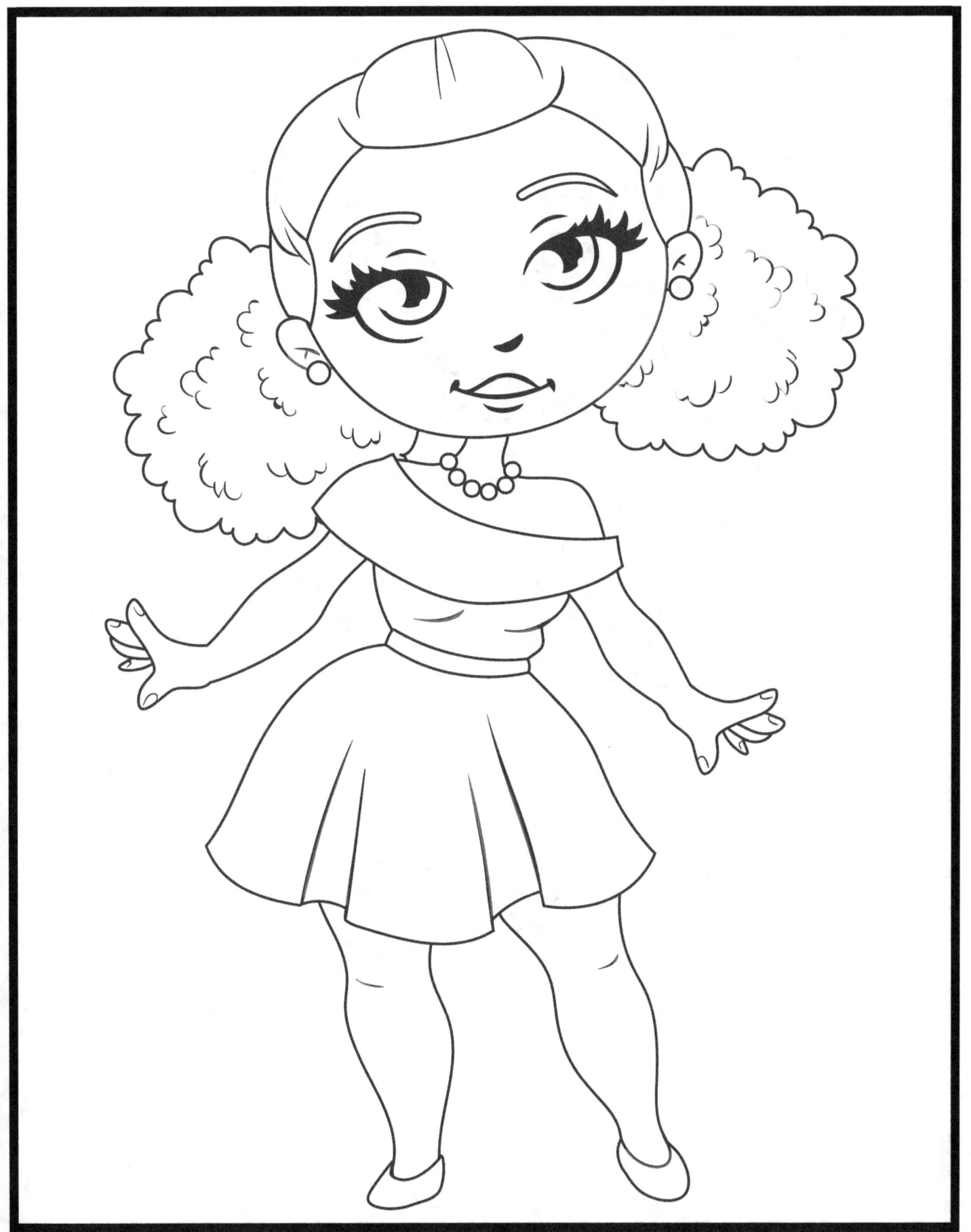

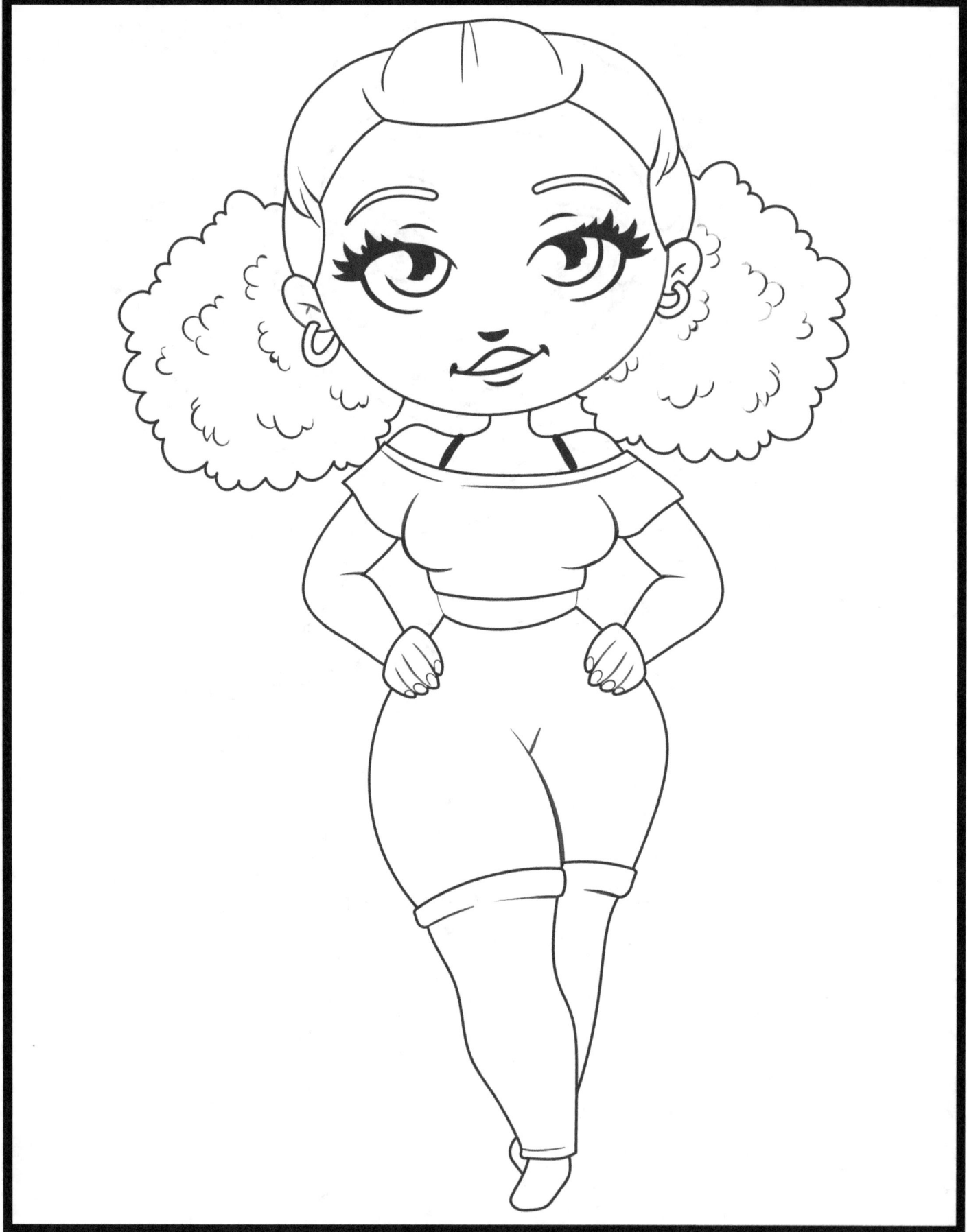

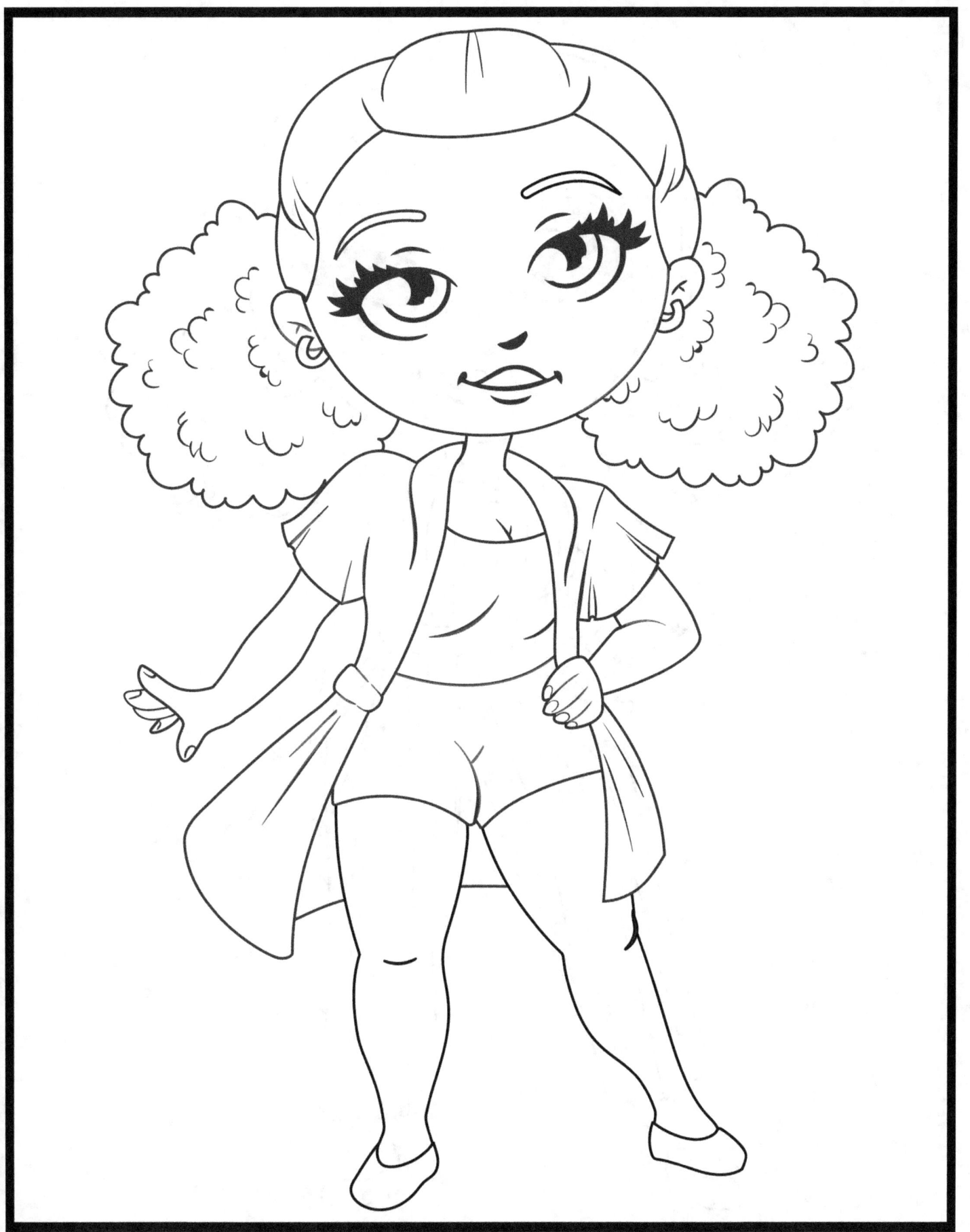

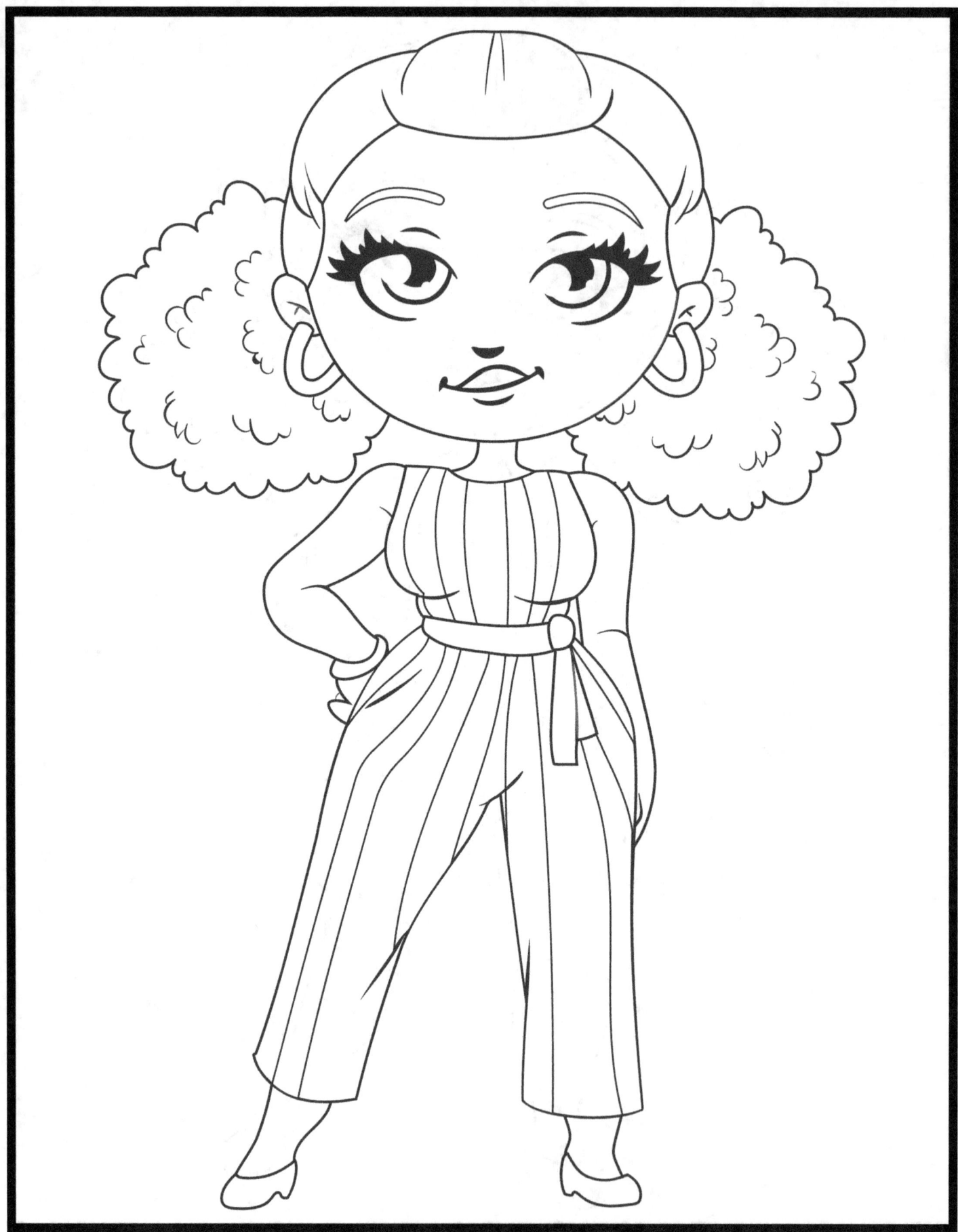

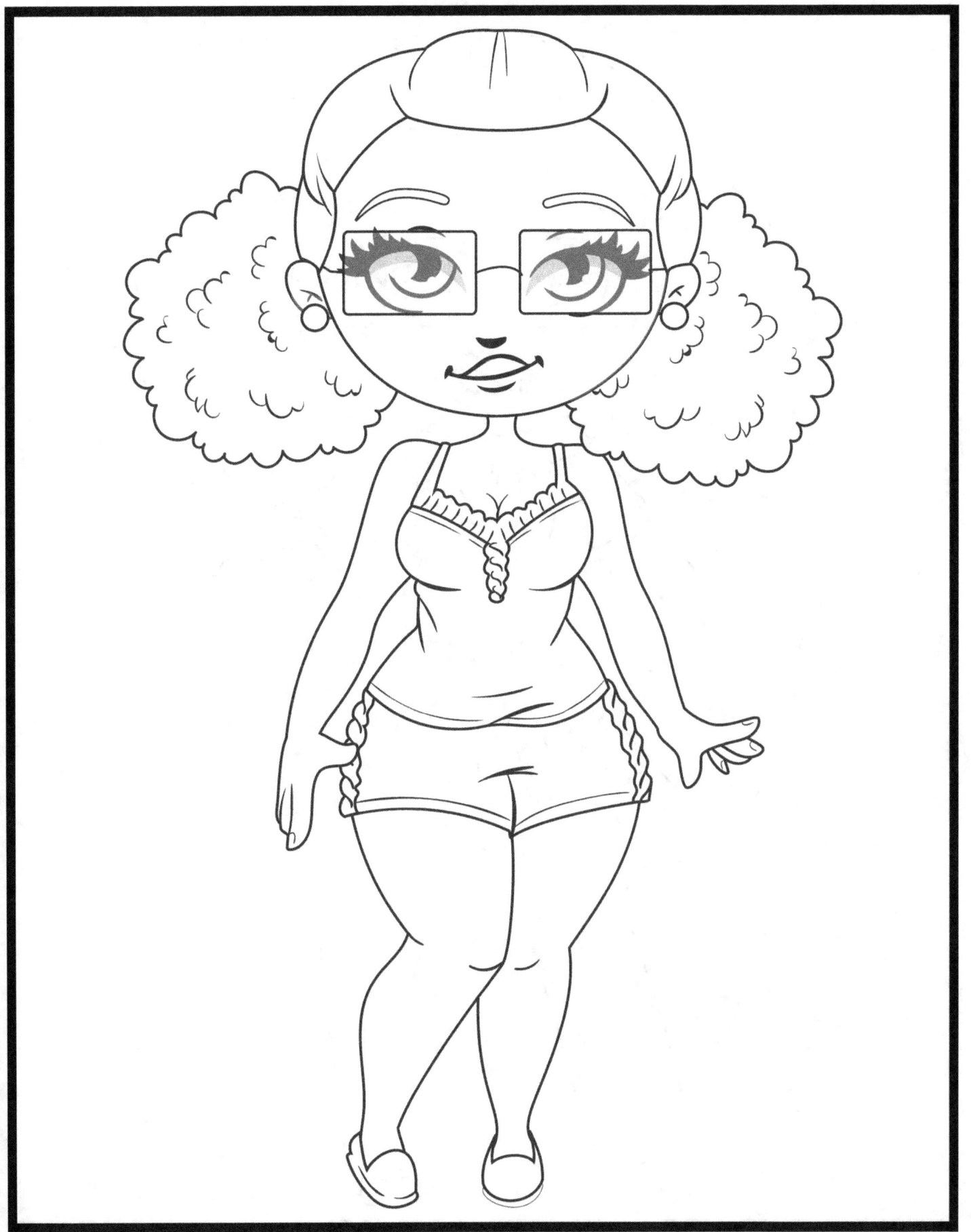

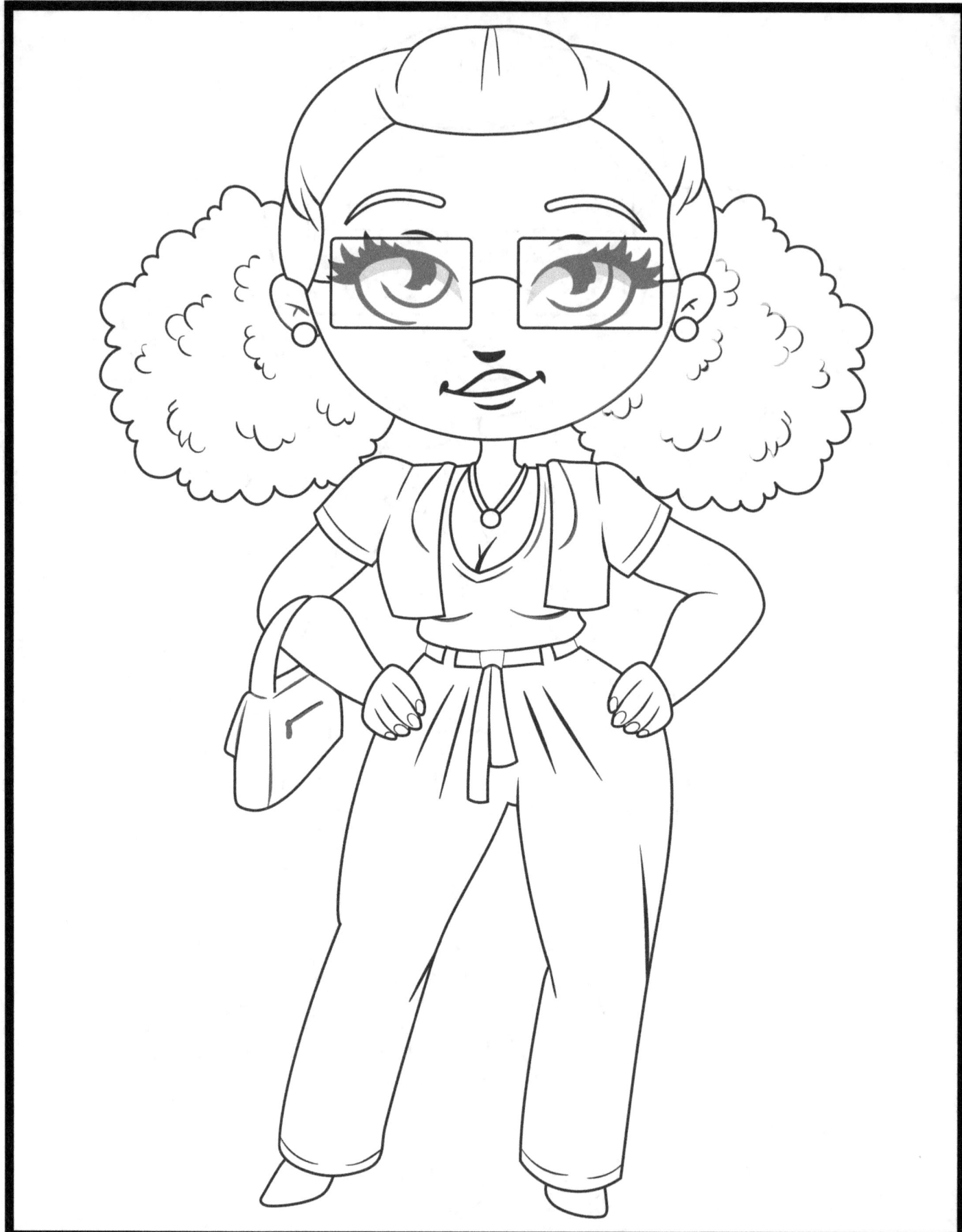

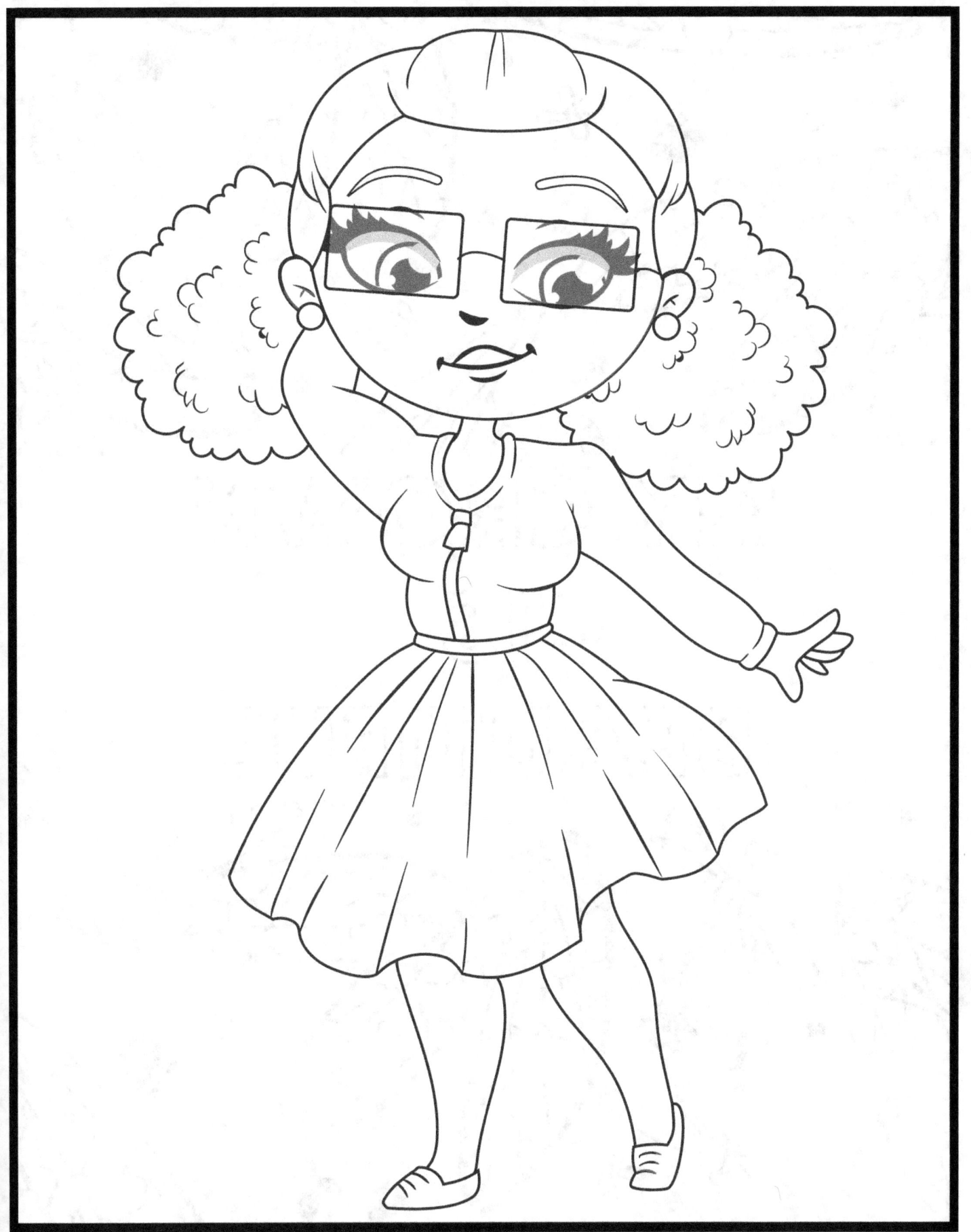

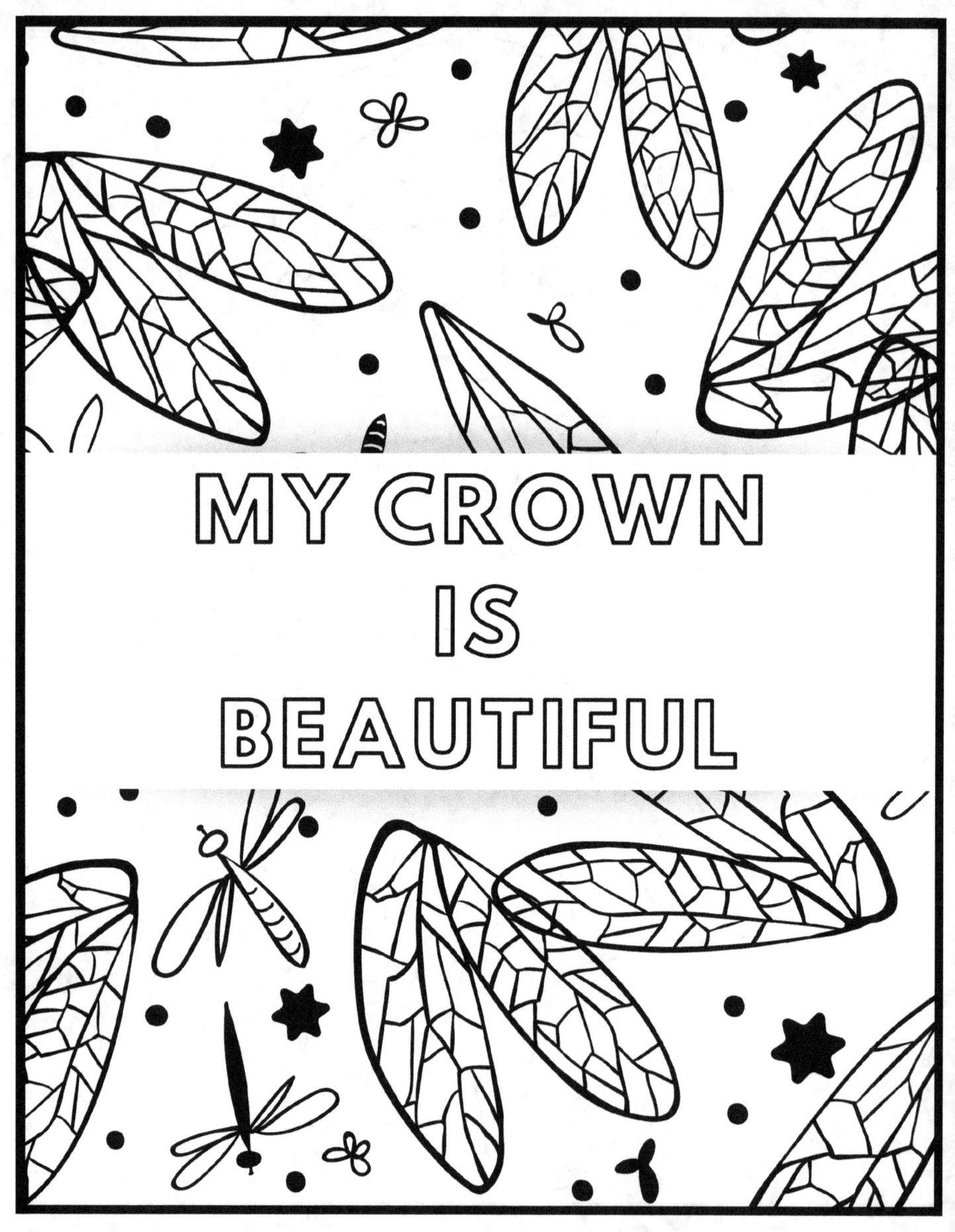

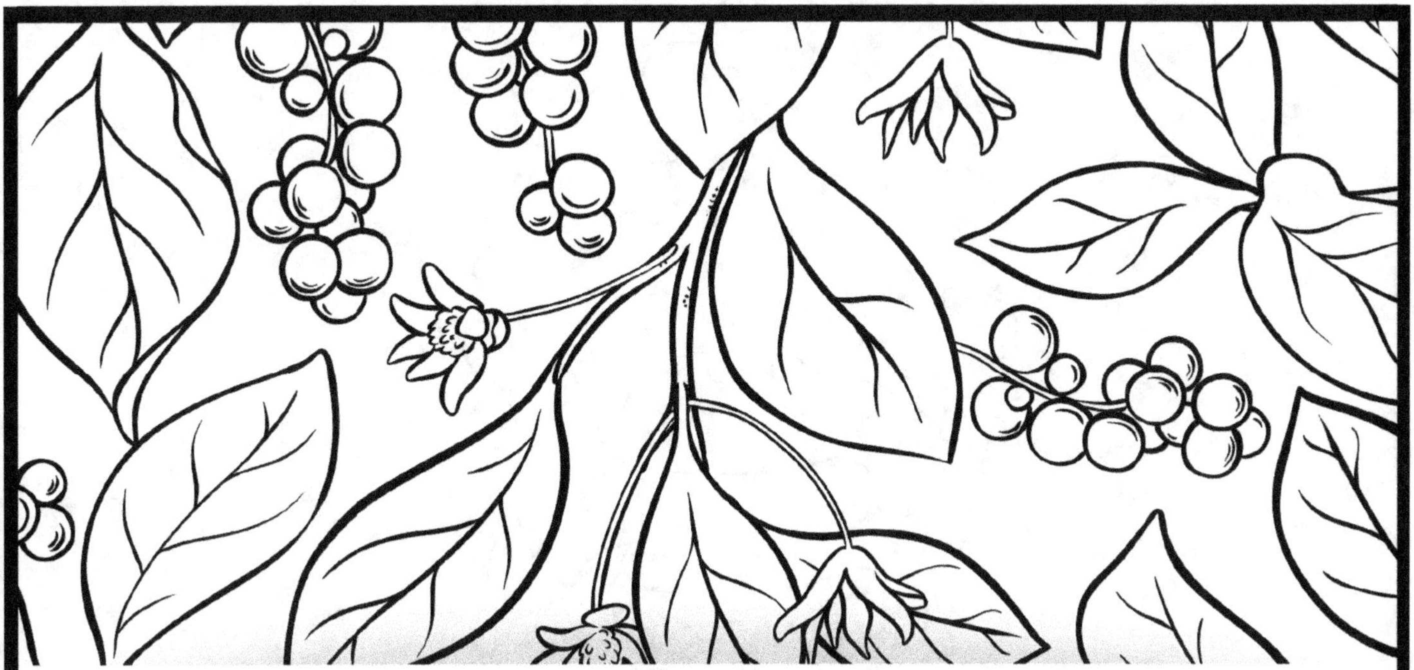

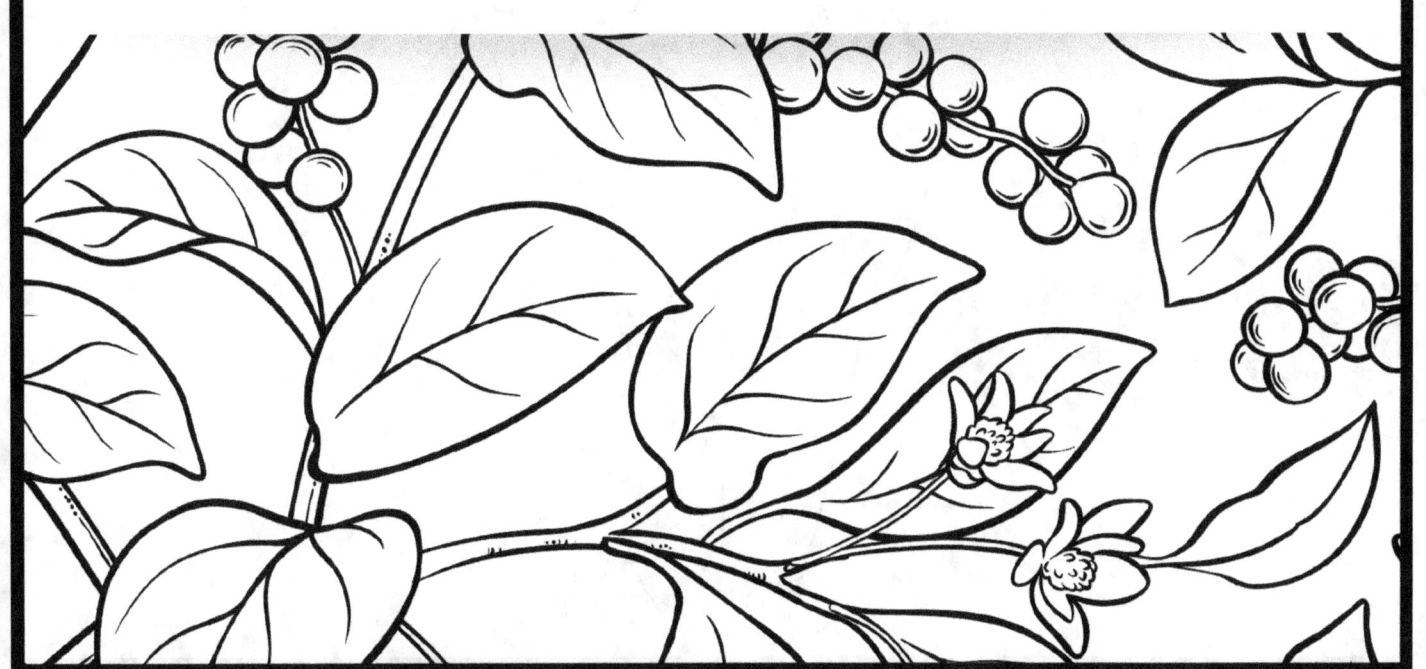
I AM BRAVE

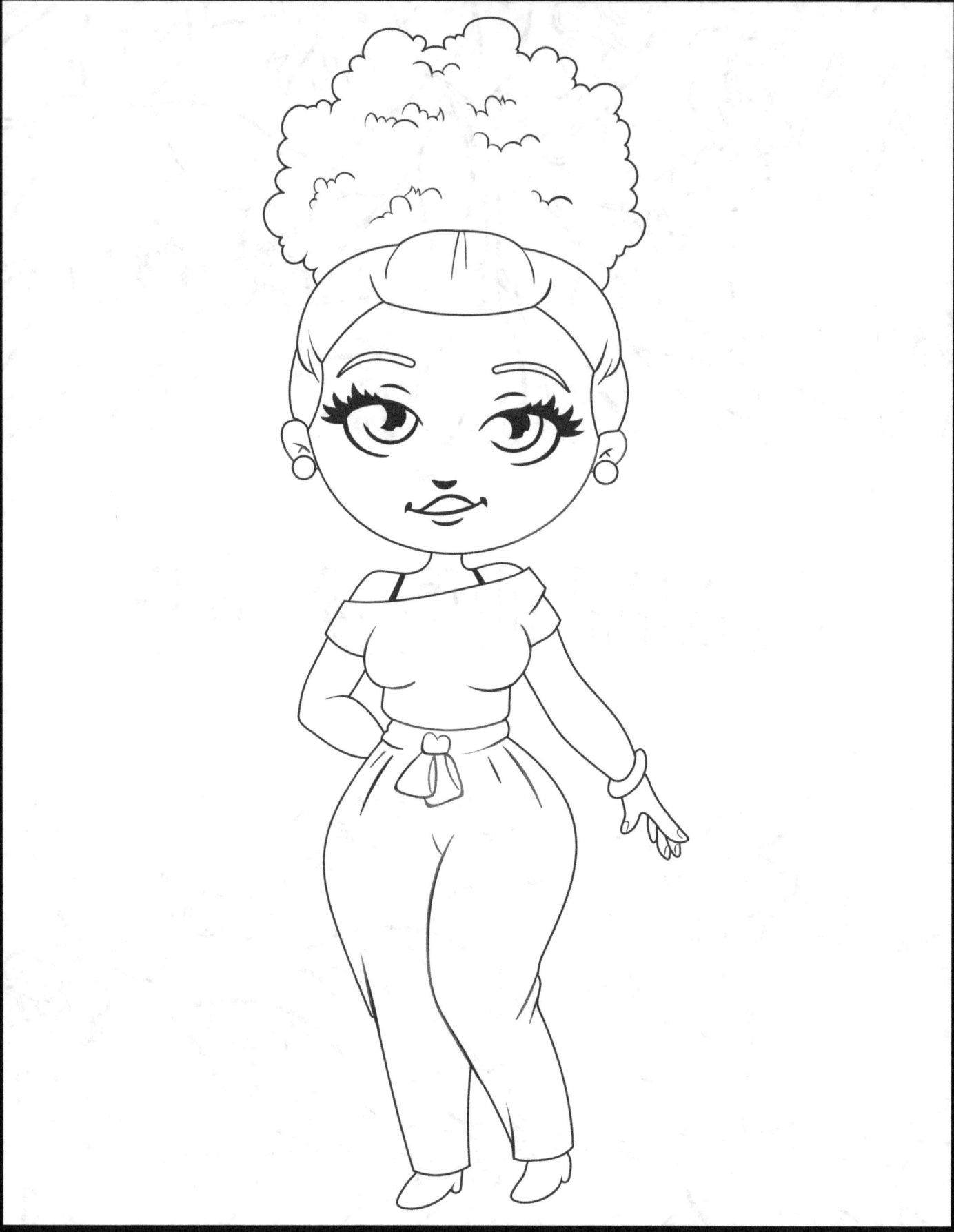

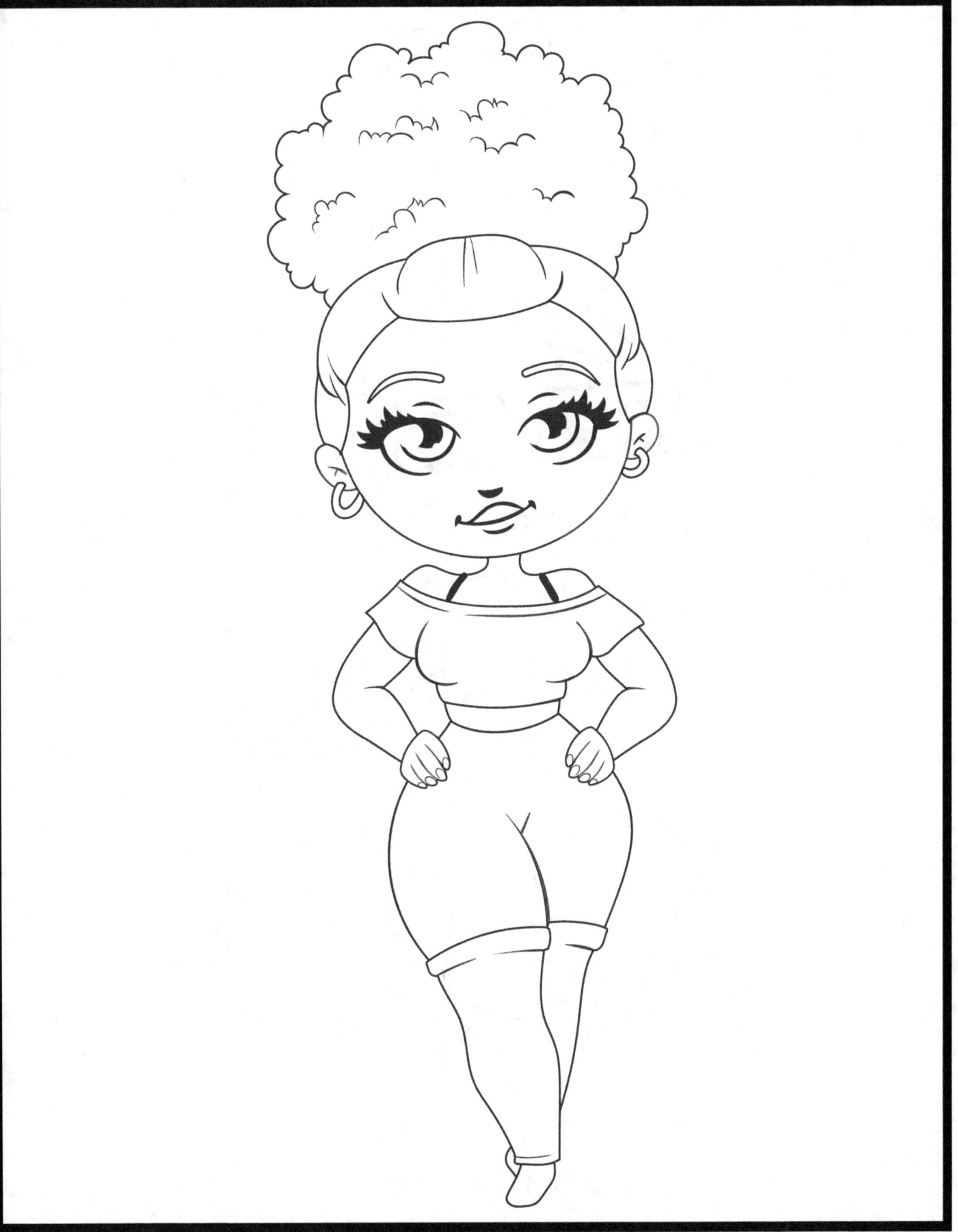

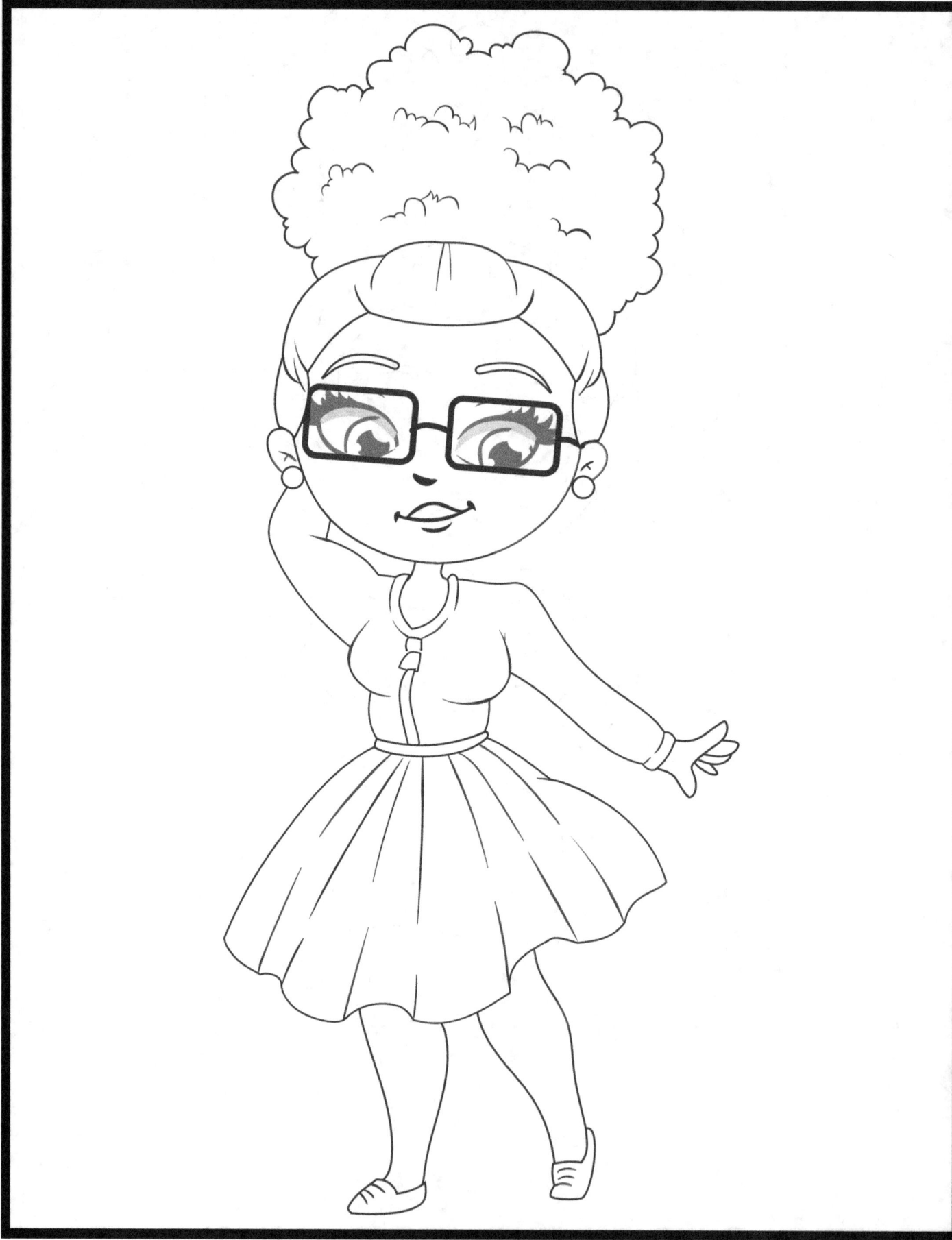

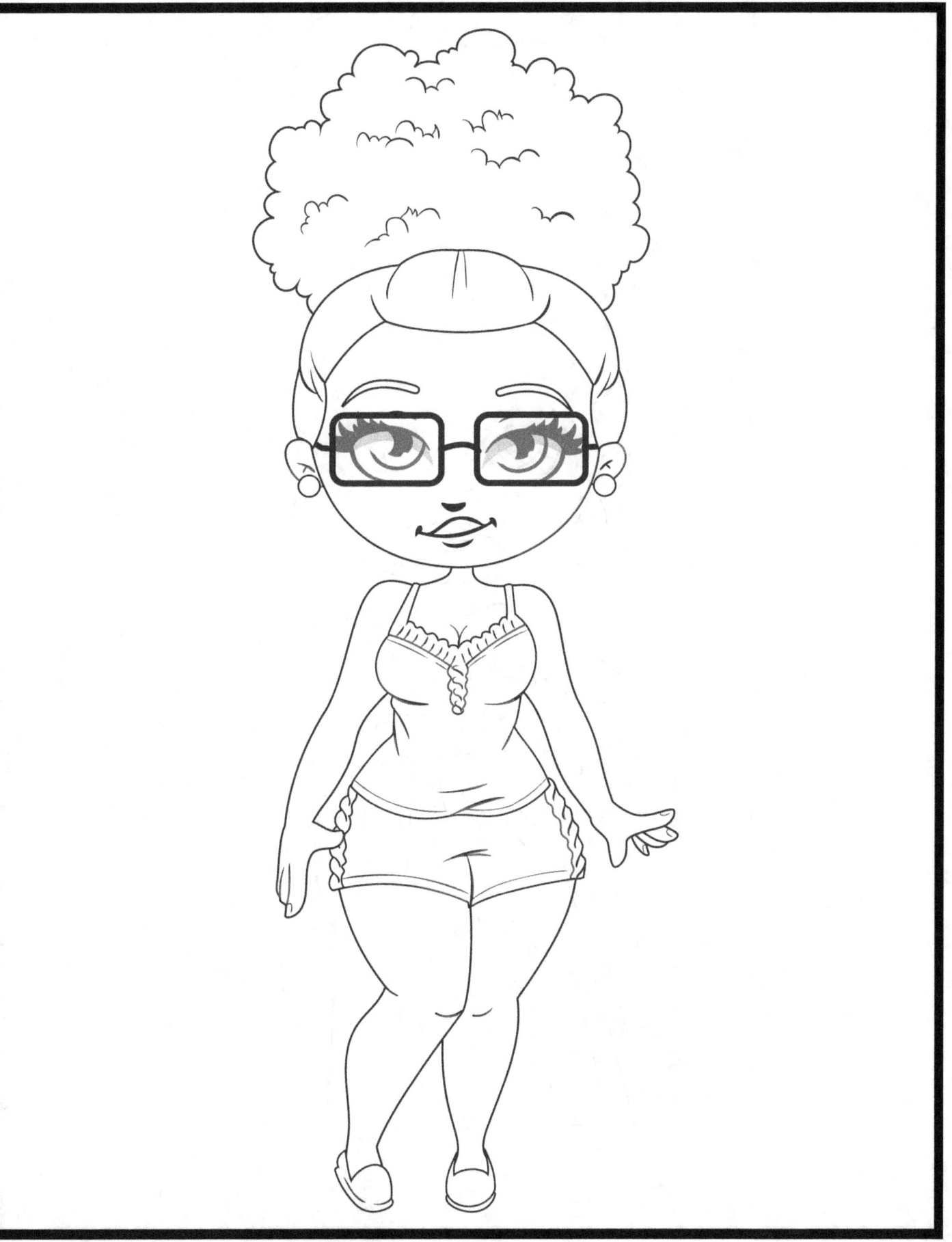

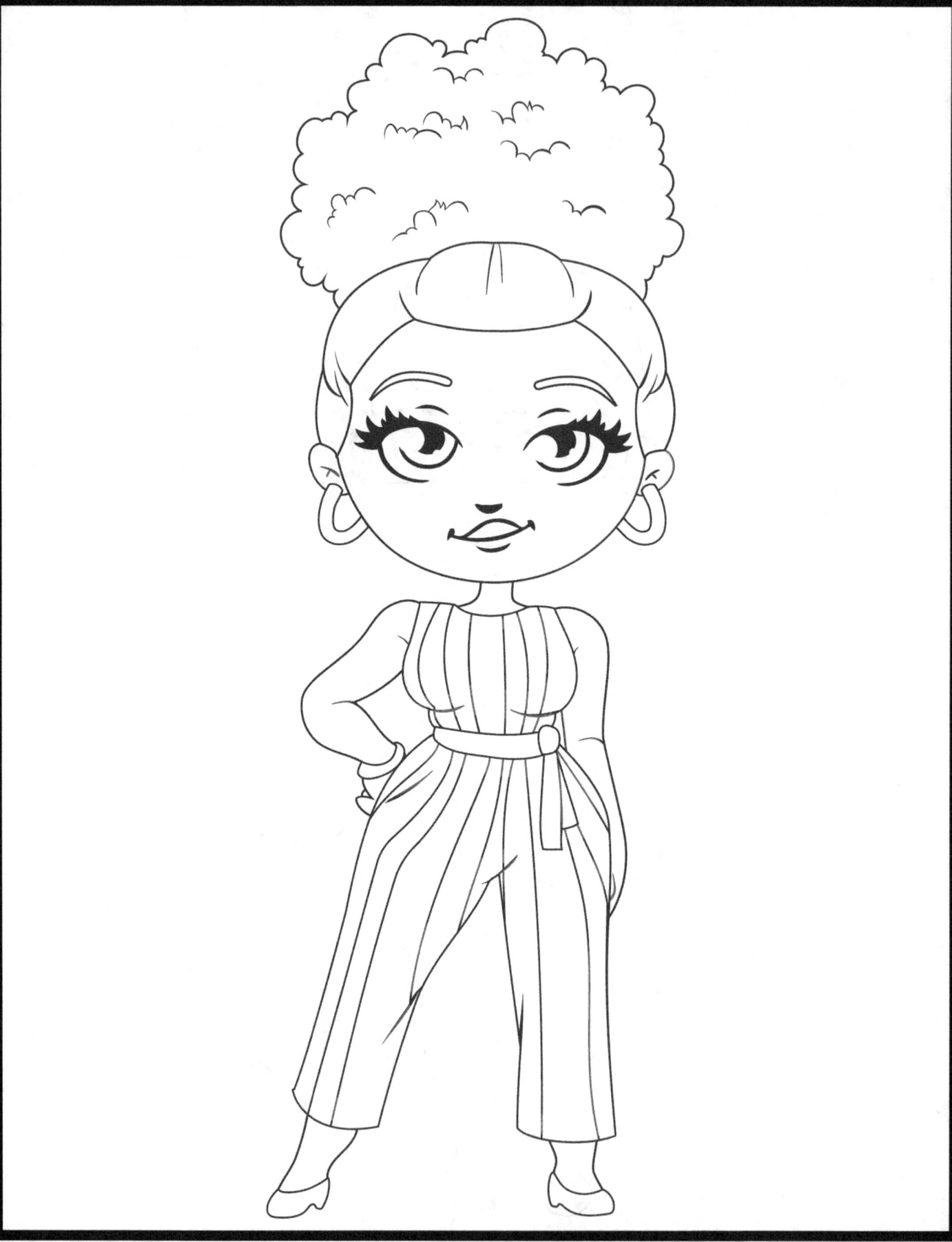

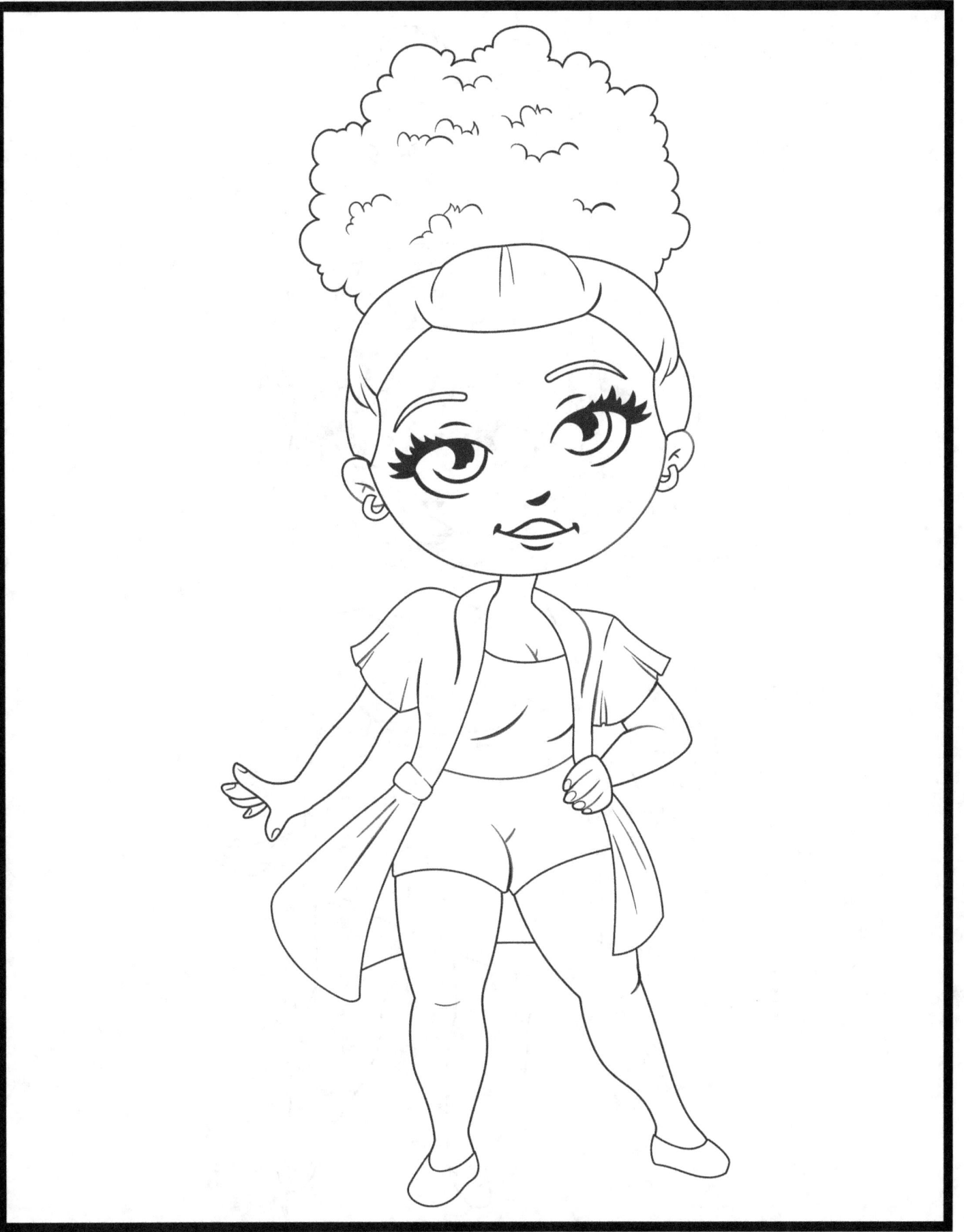

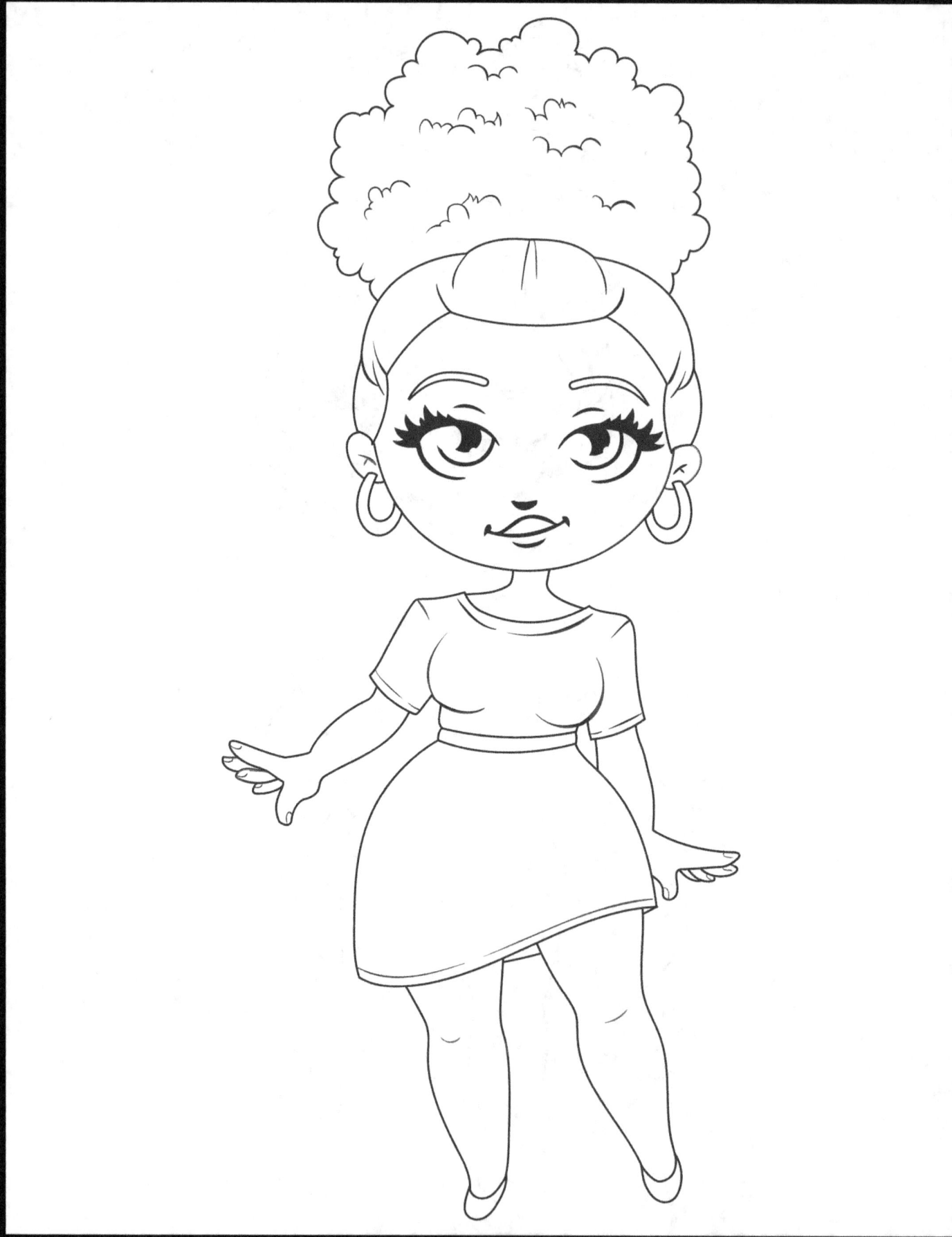

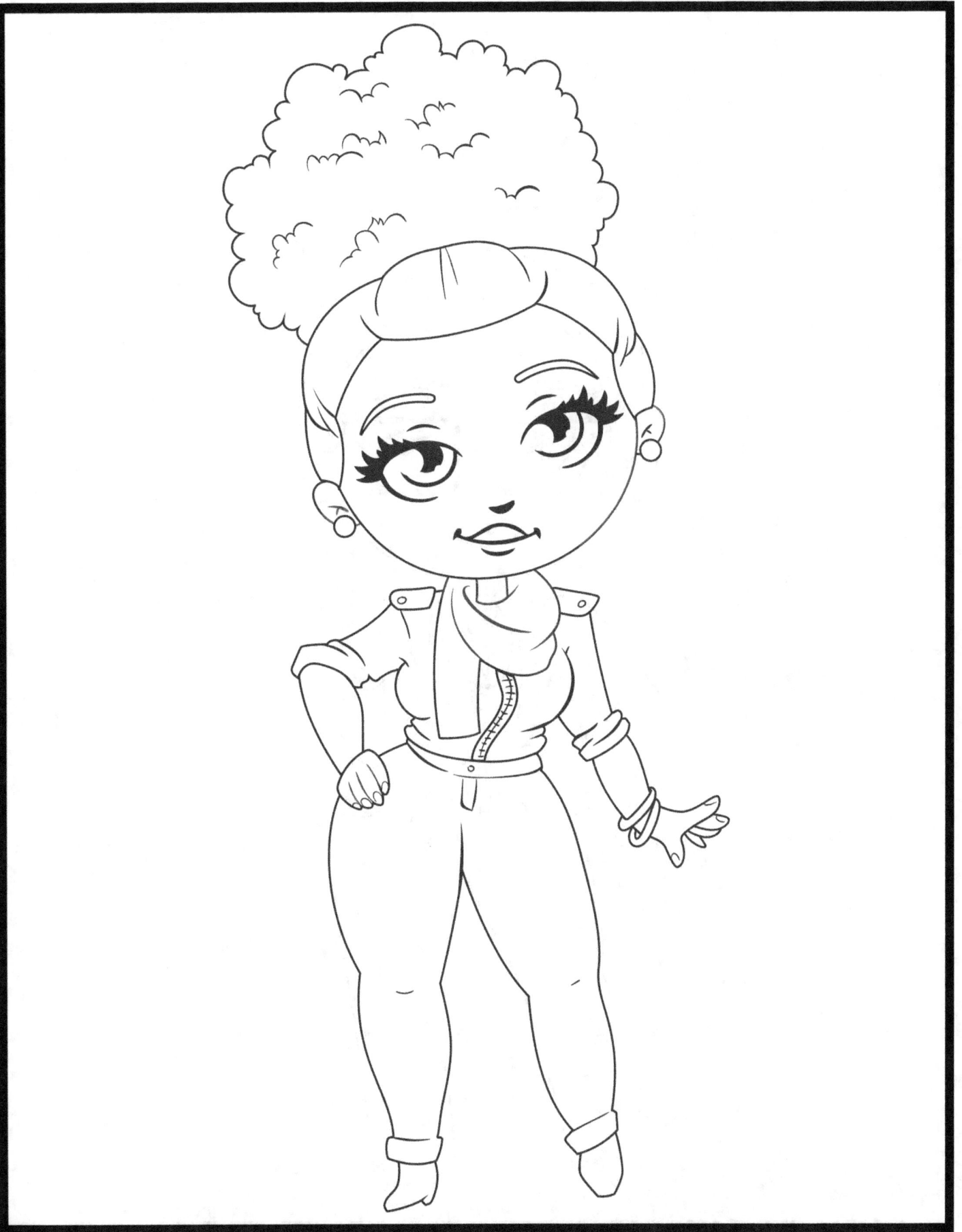

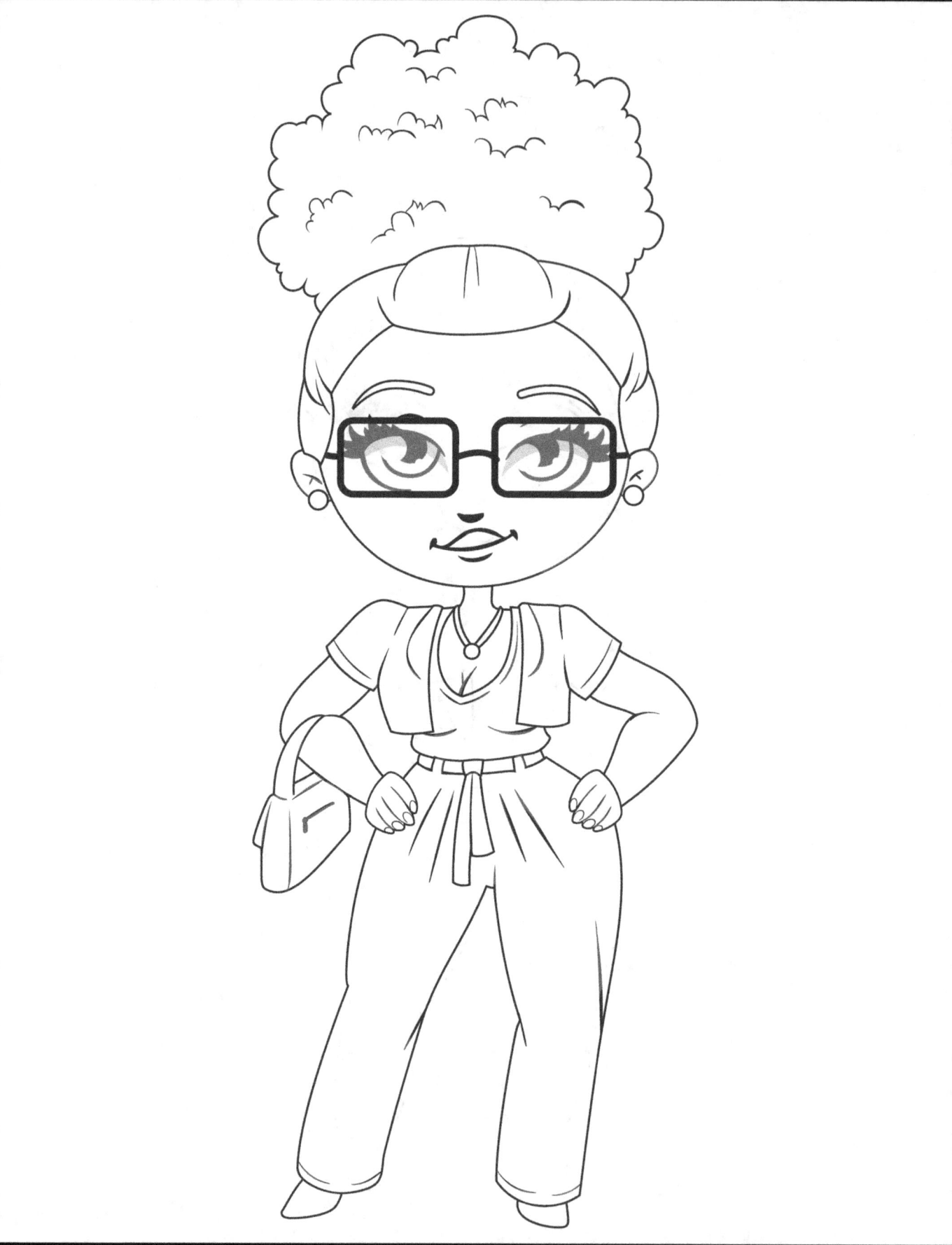

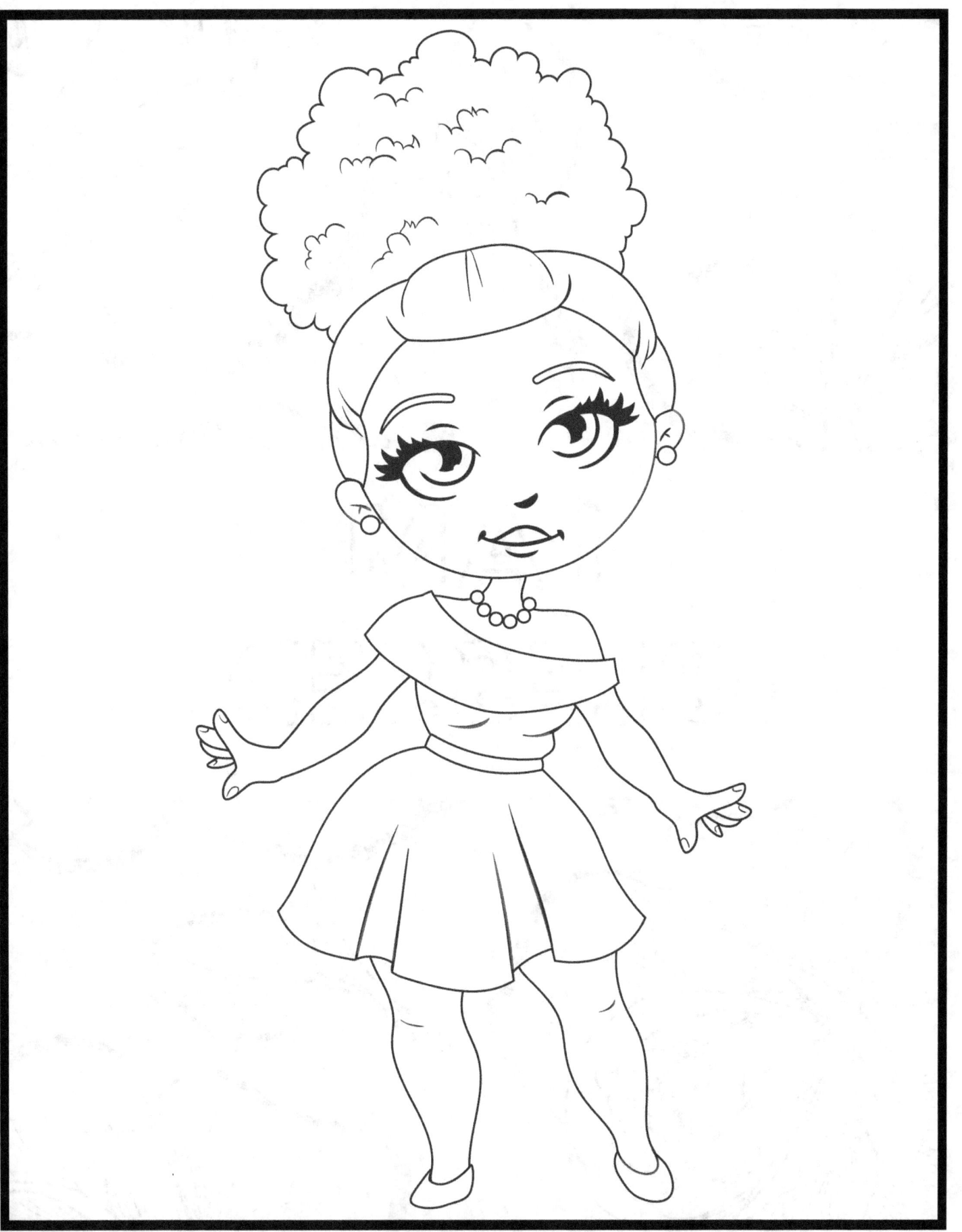

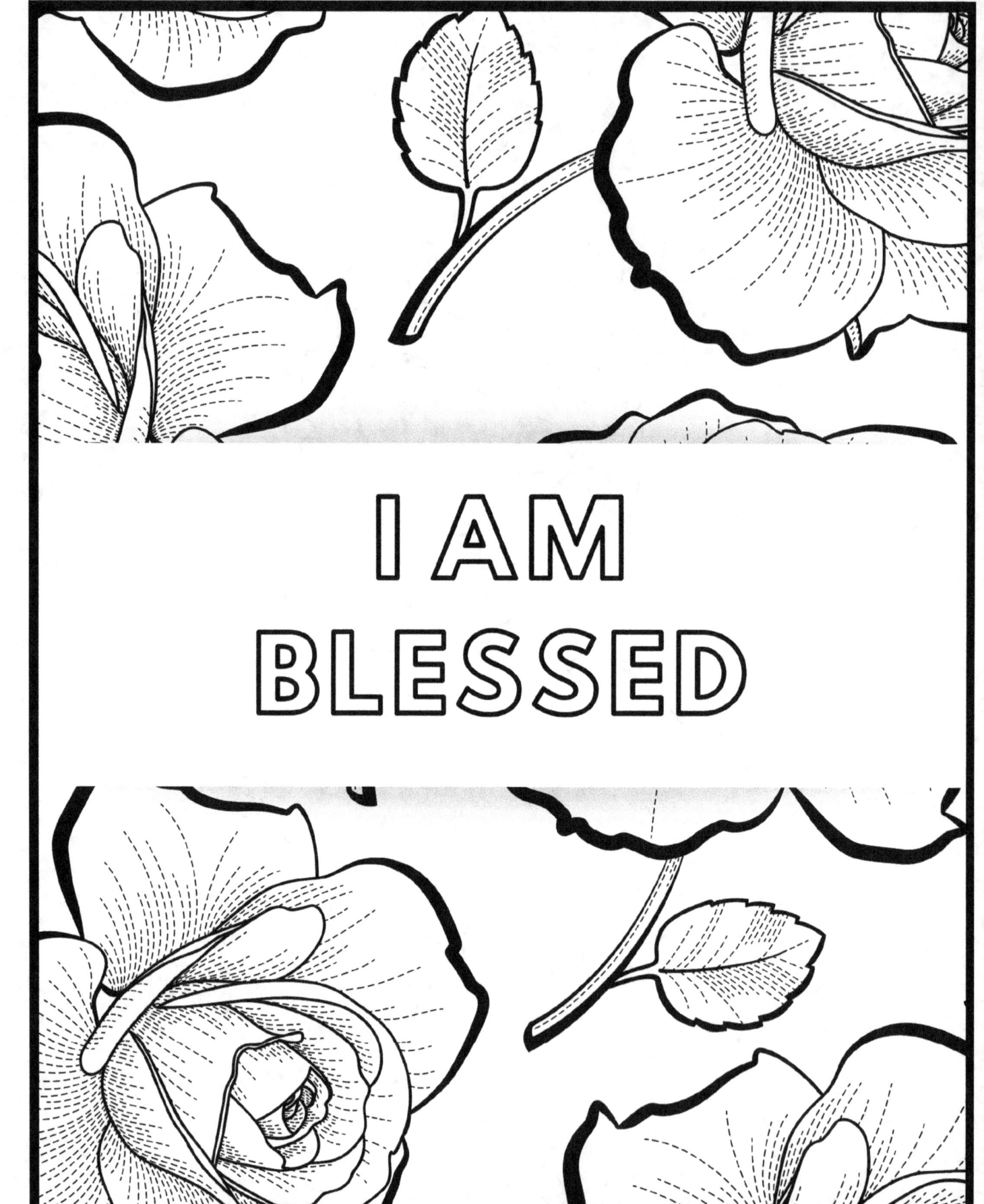

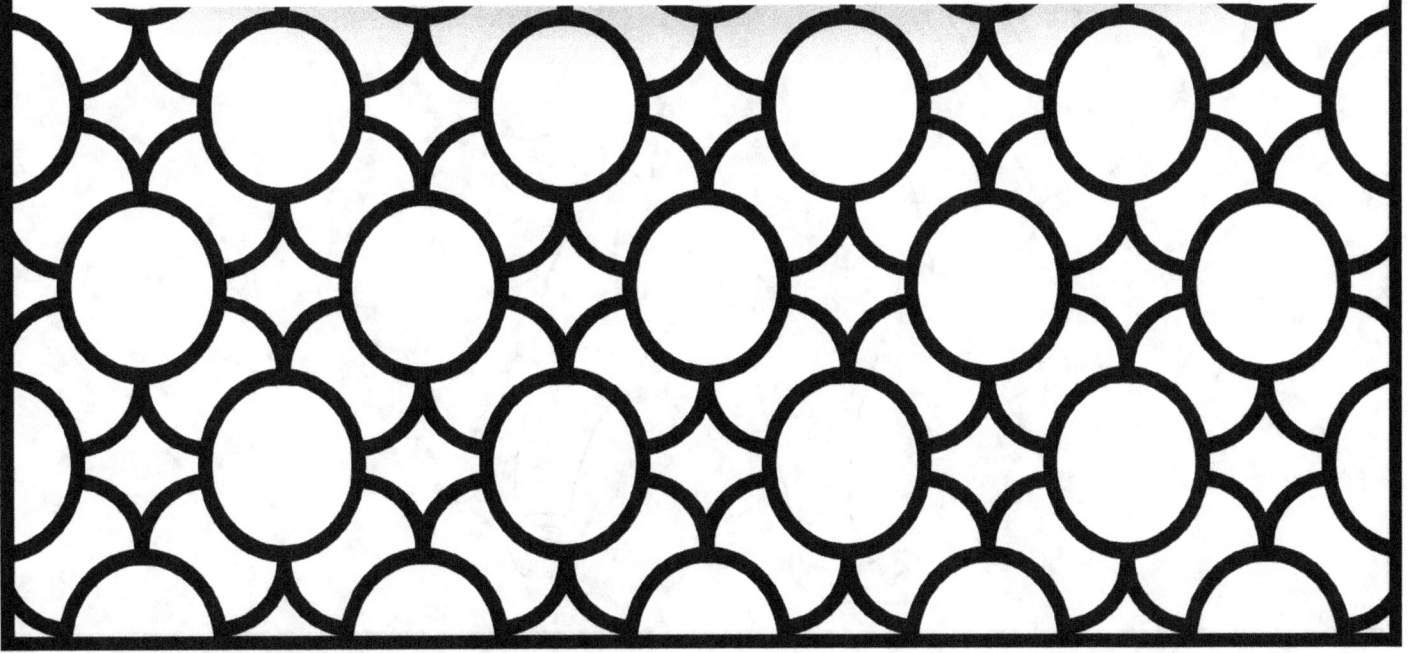

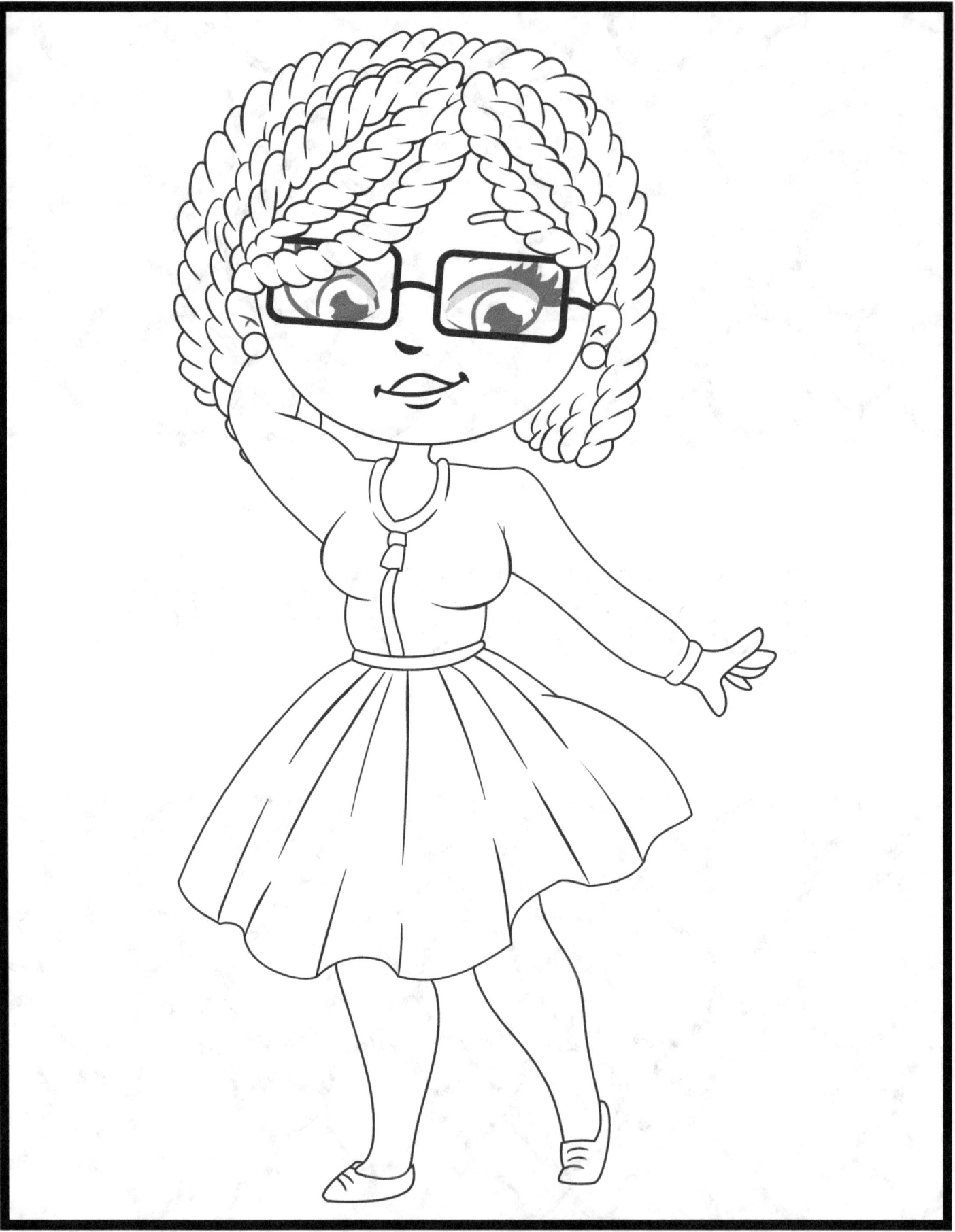

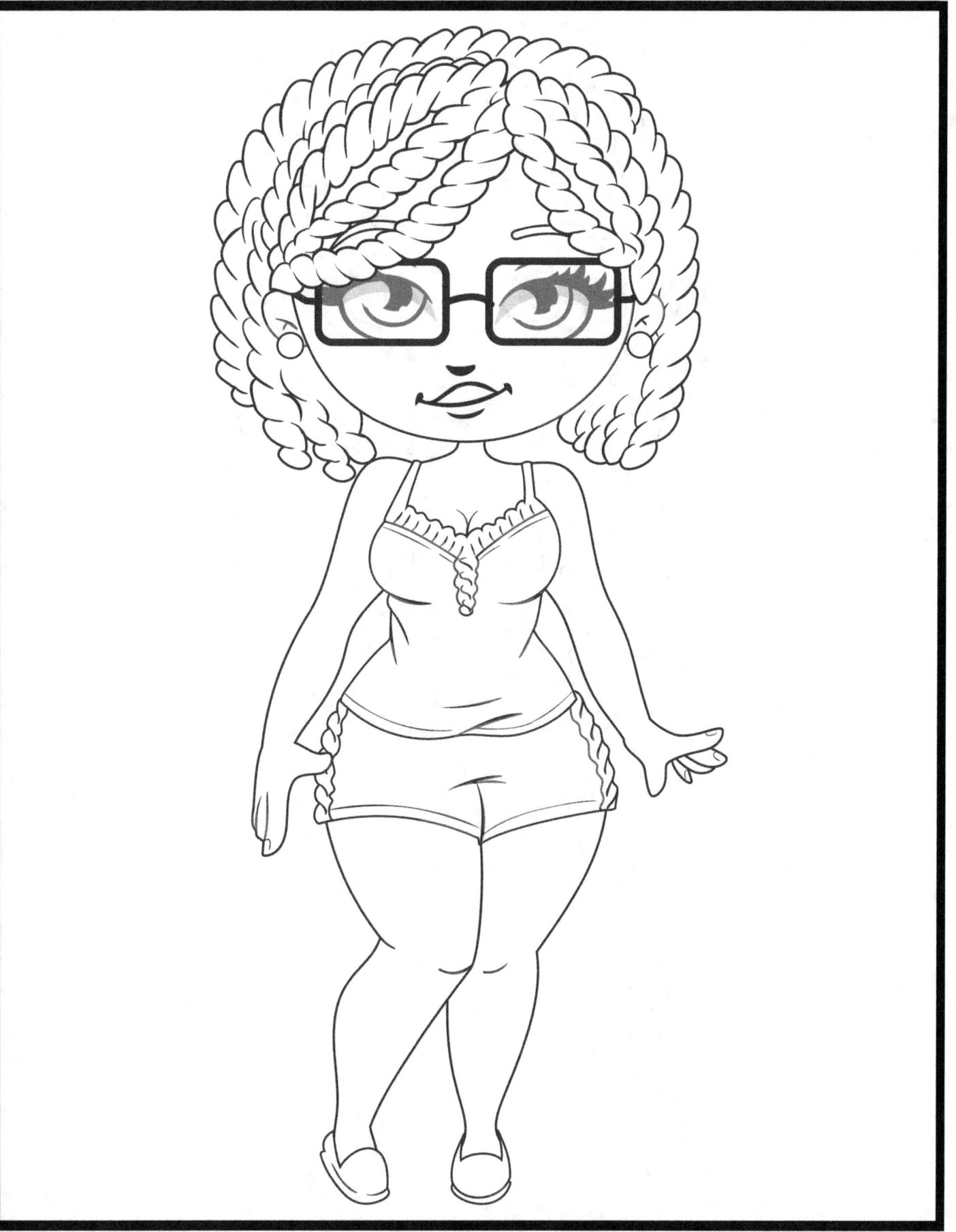

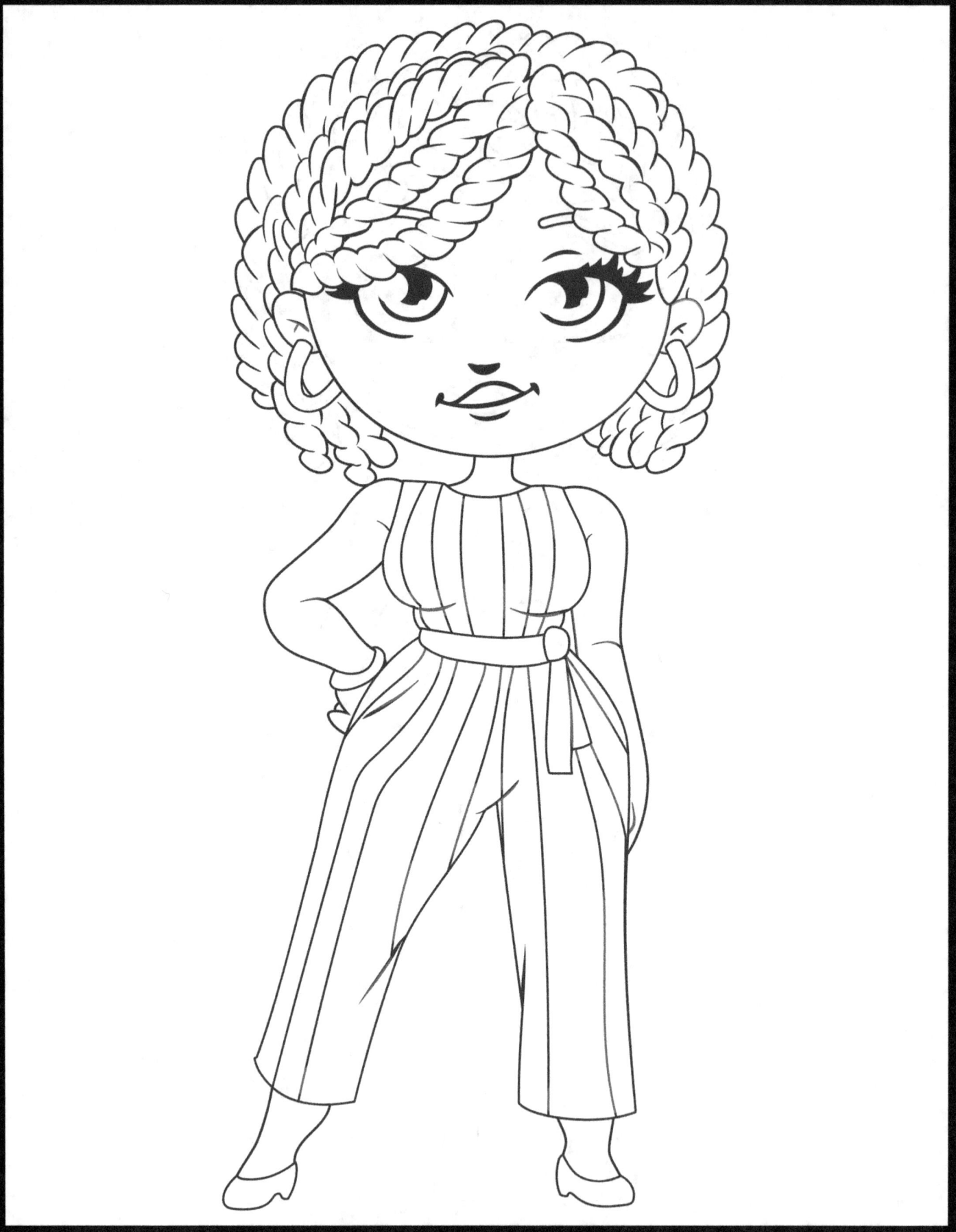

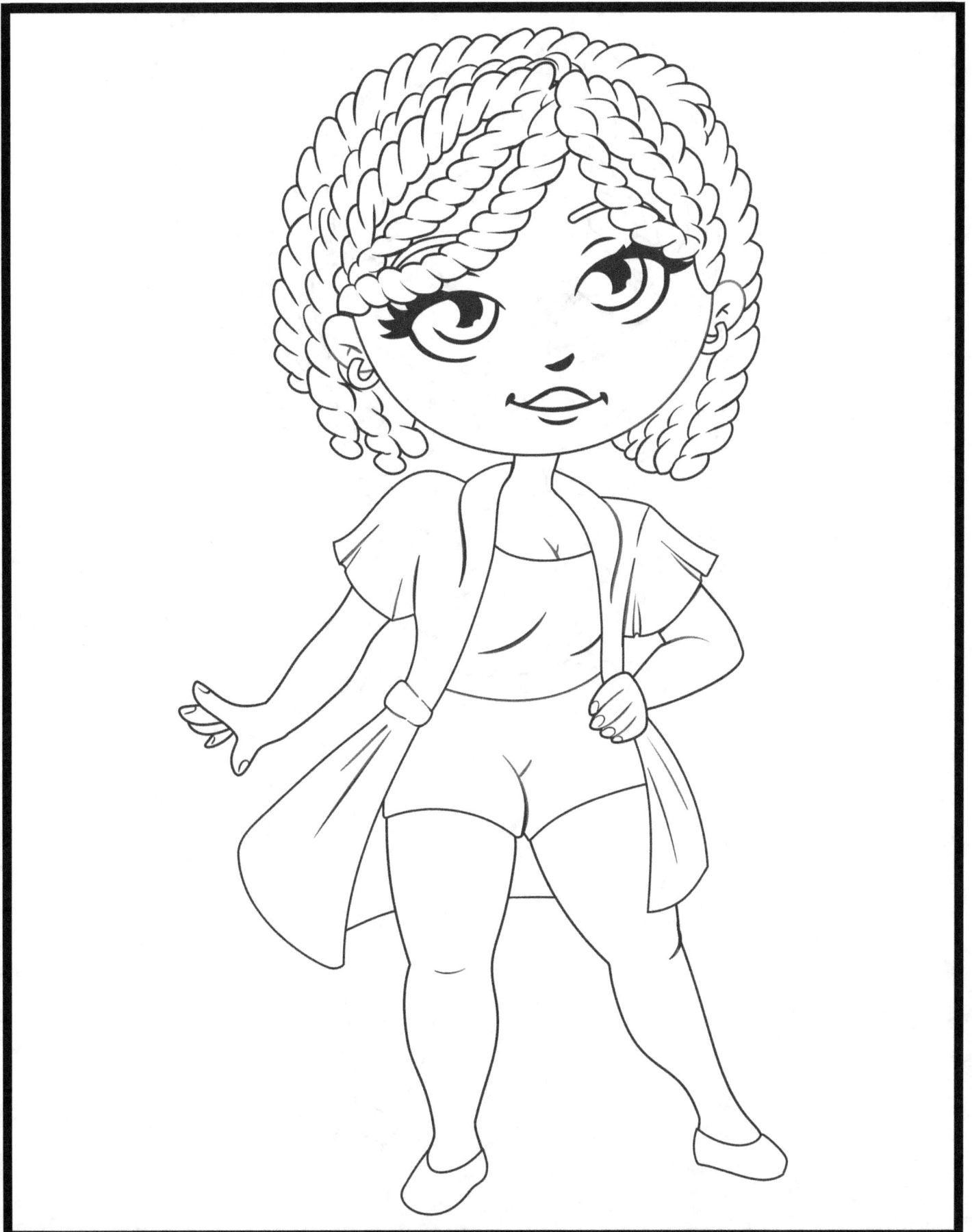

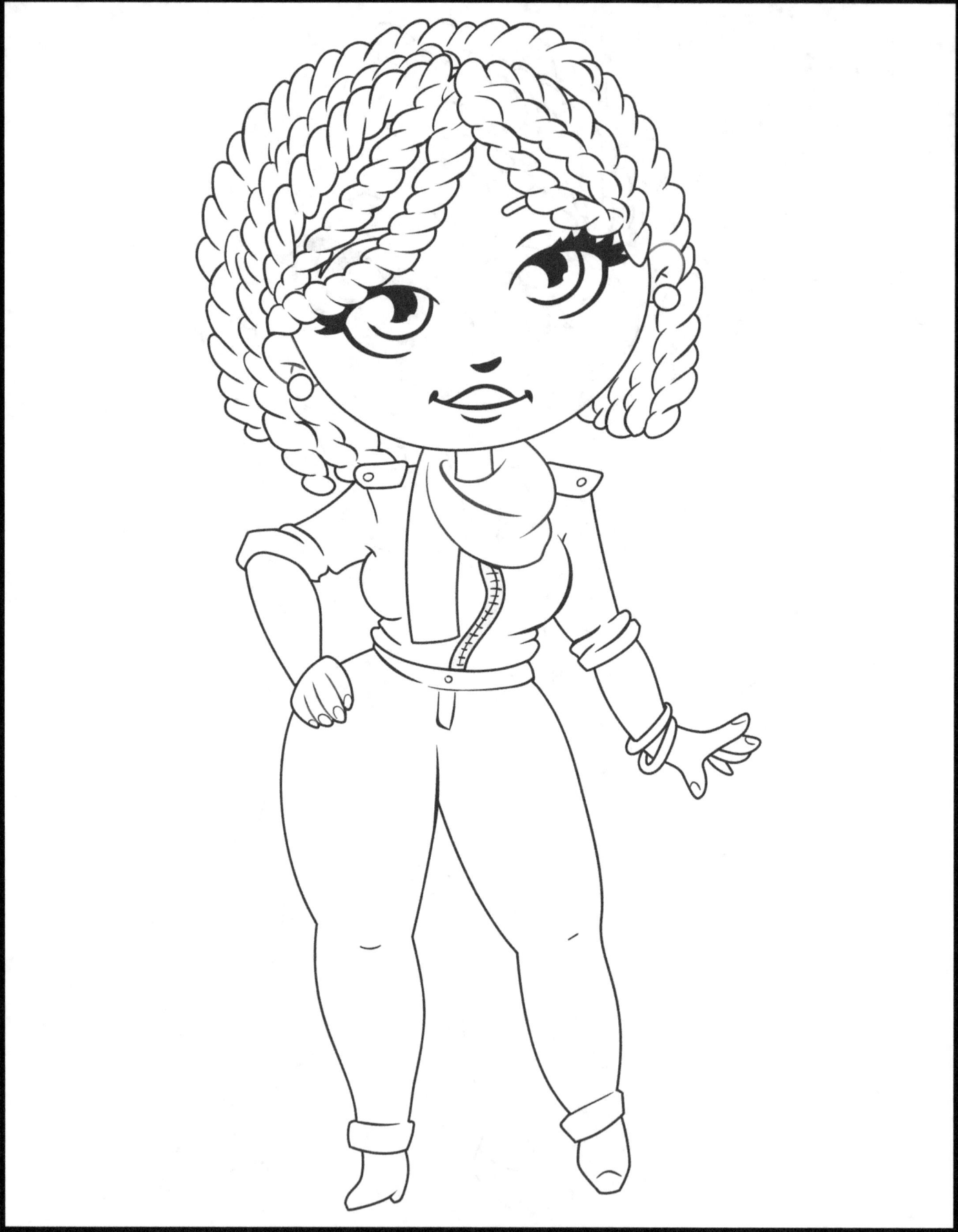

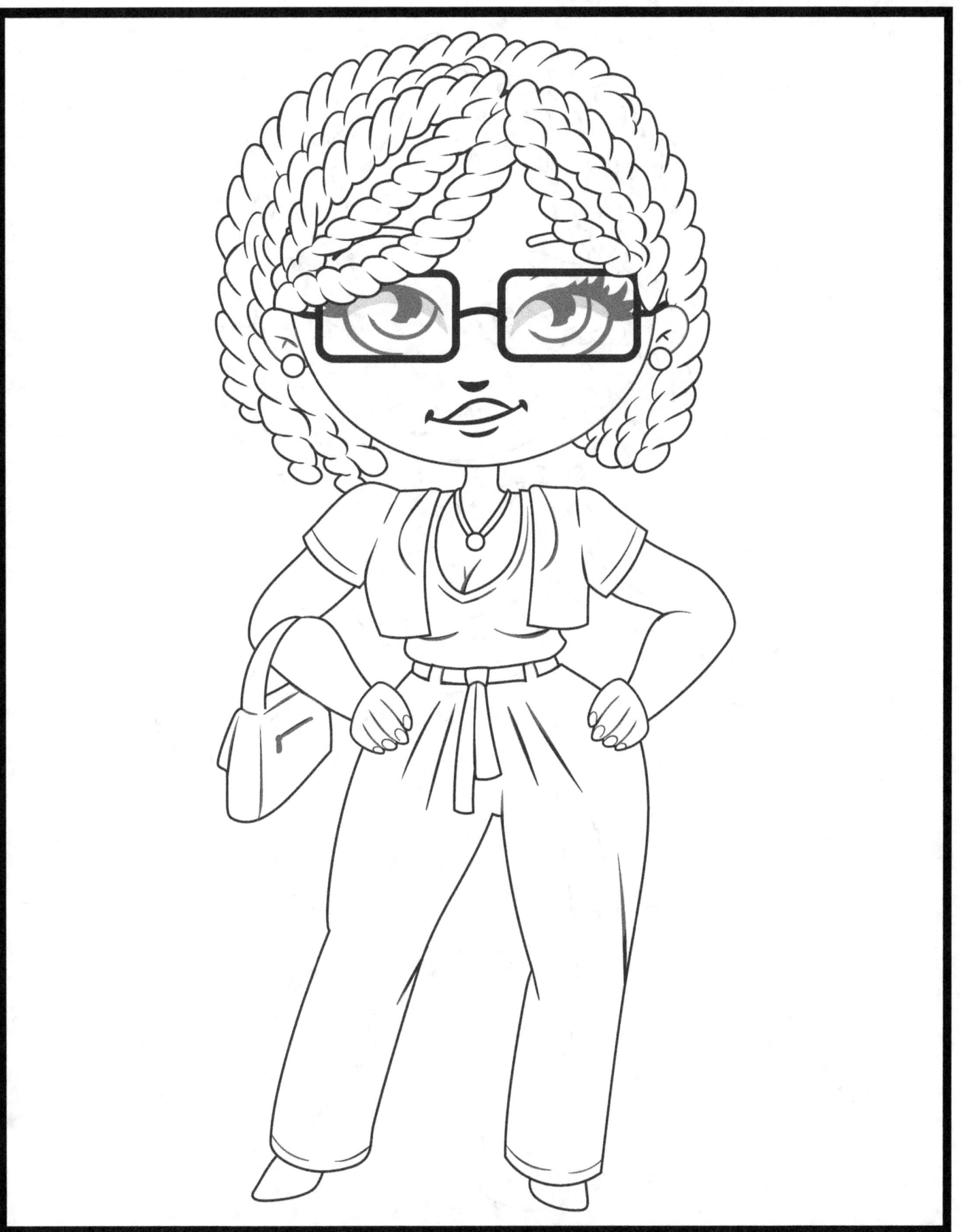

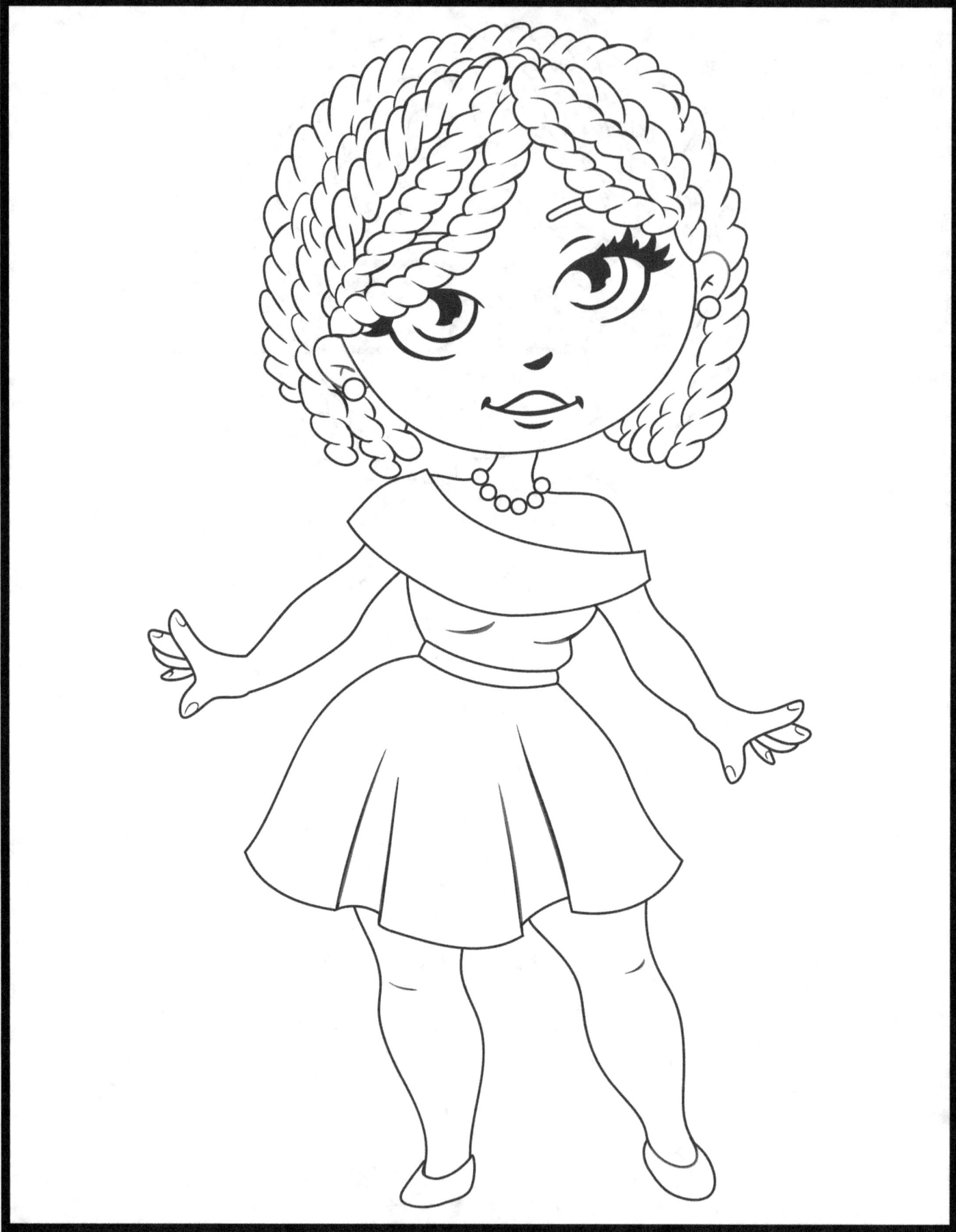

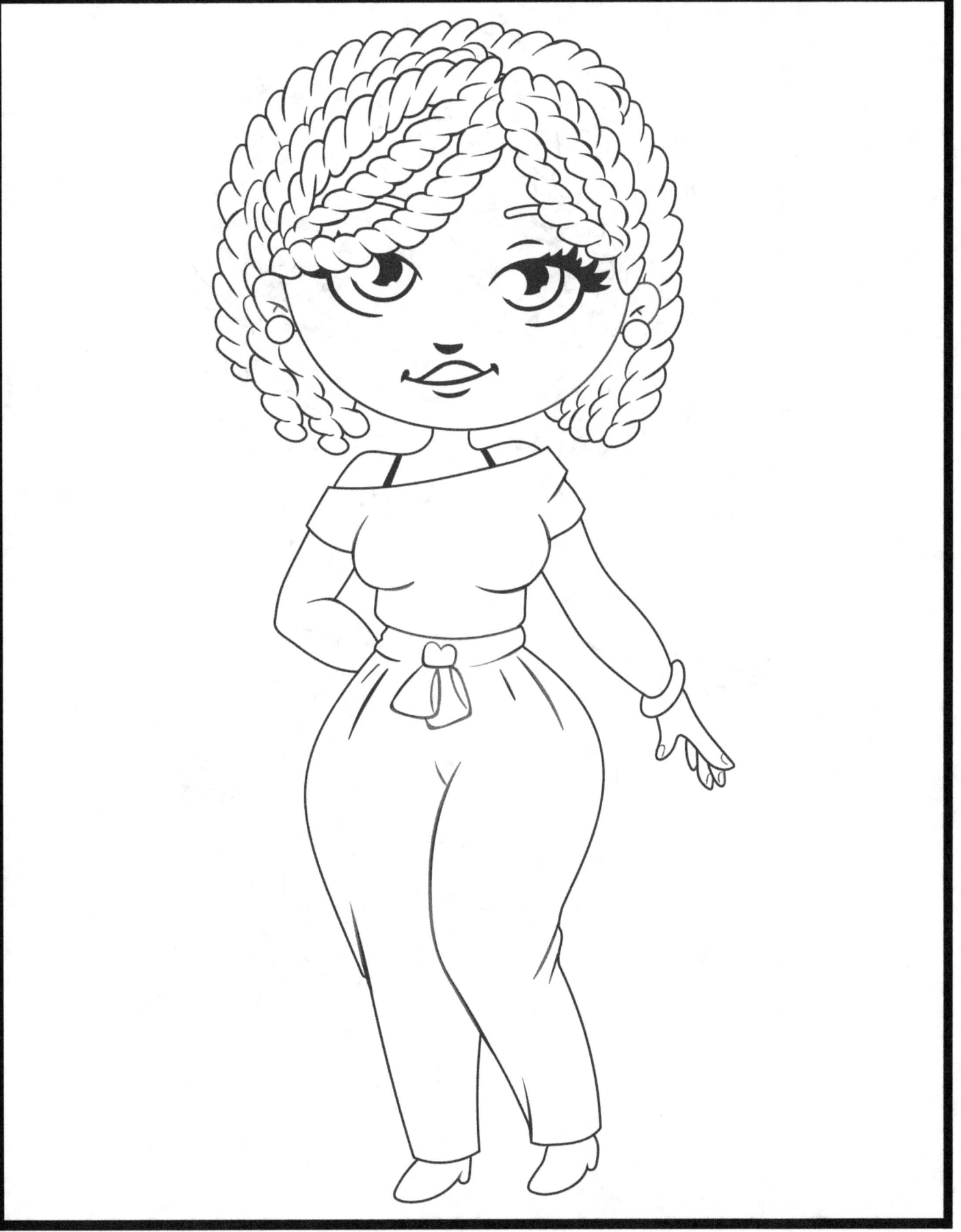

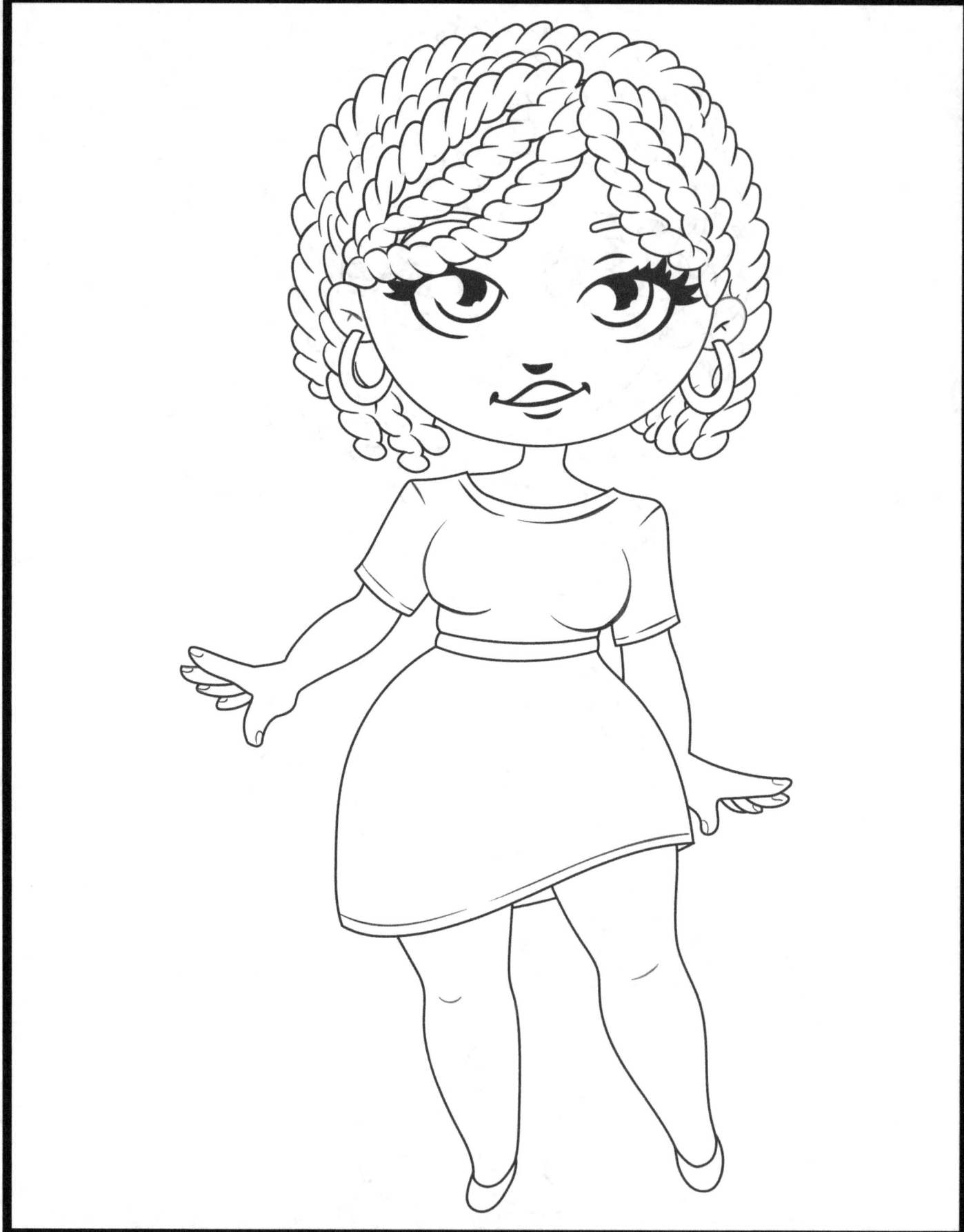

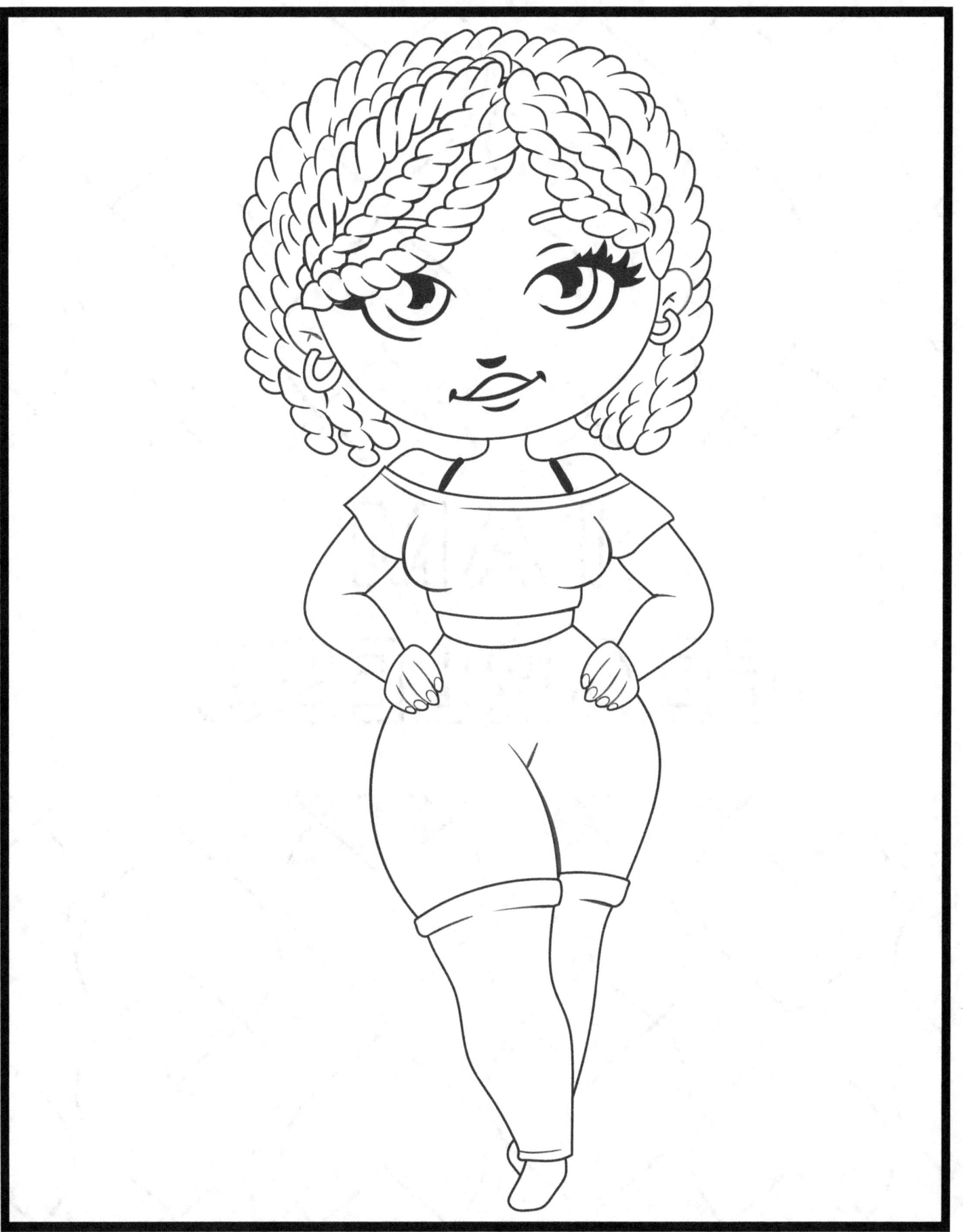

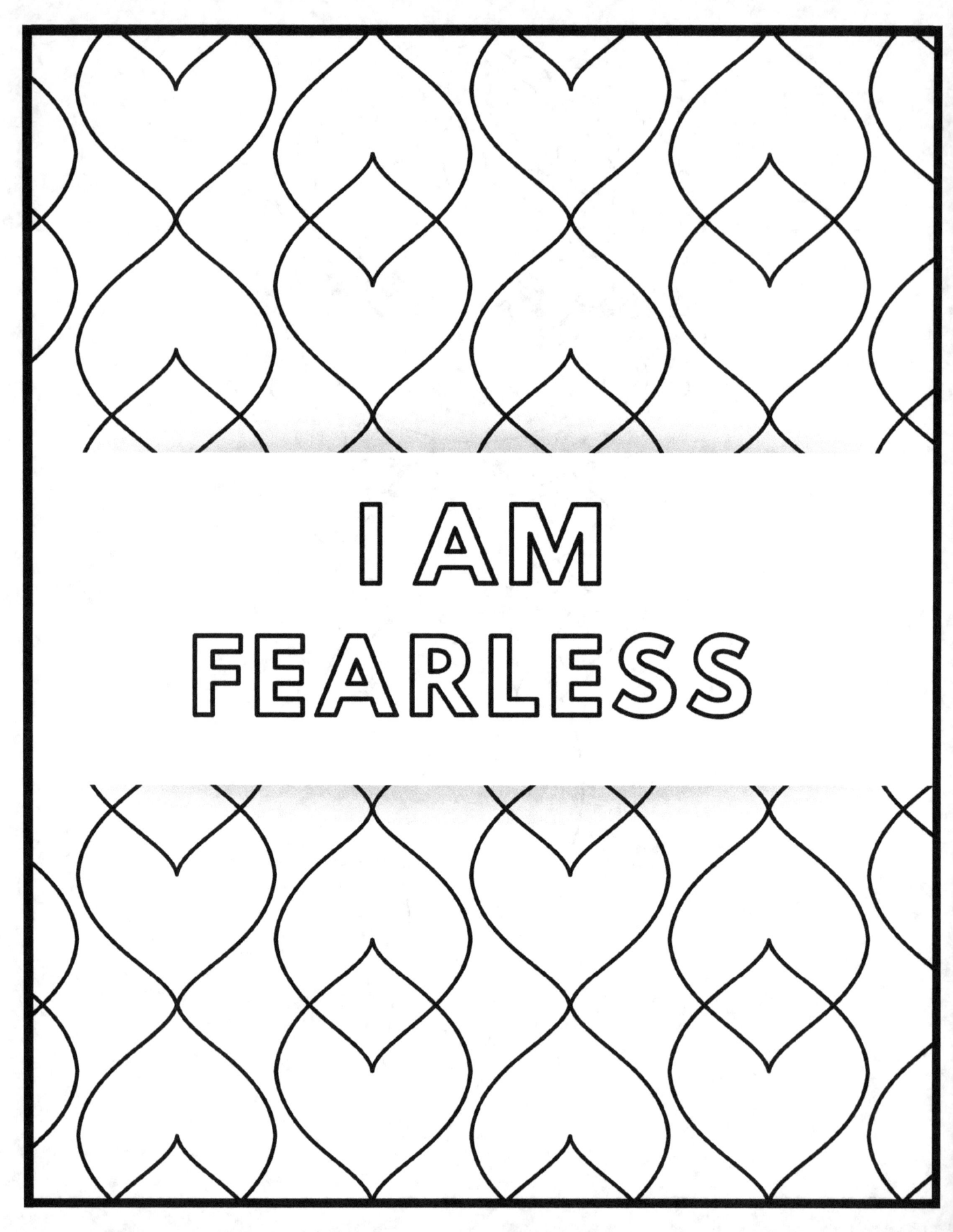

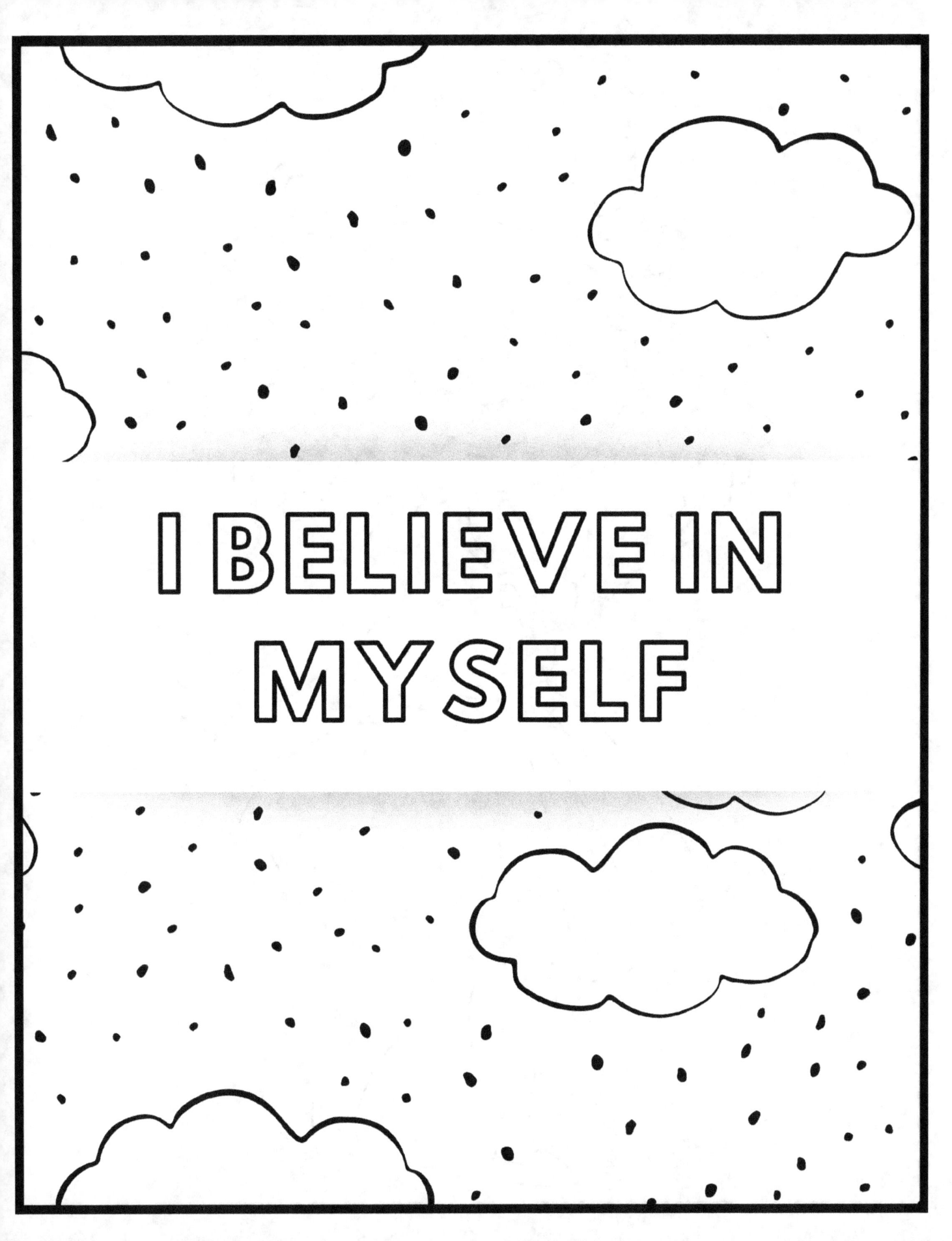

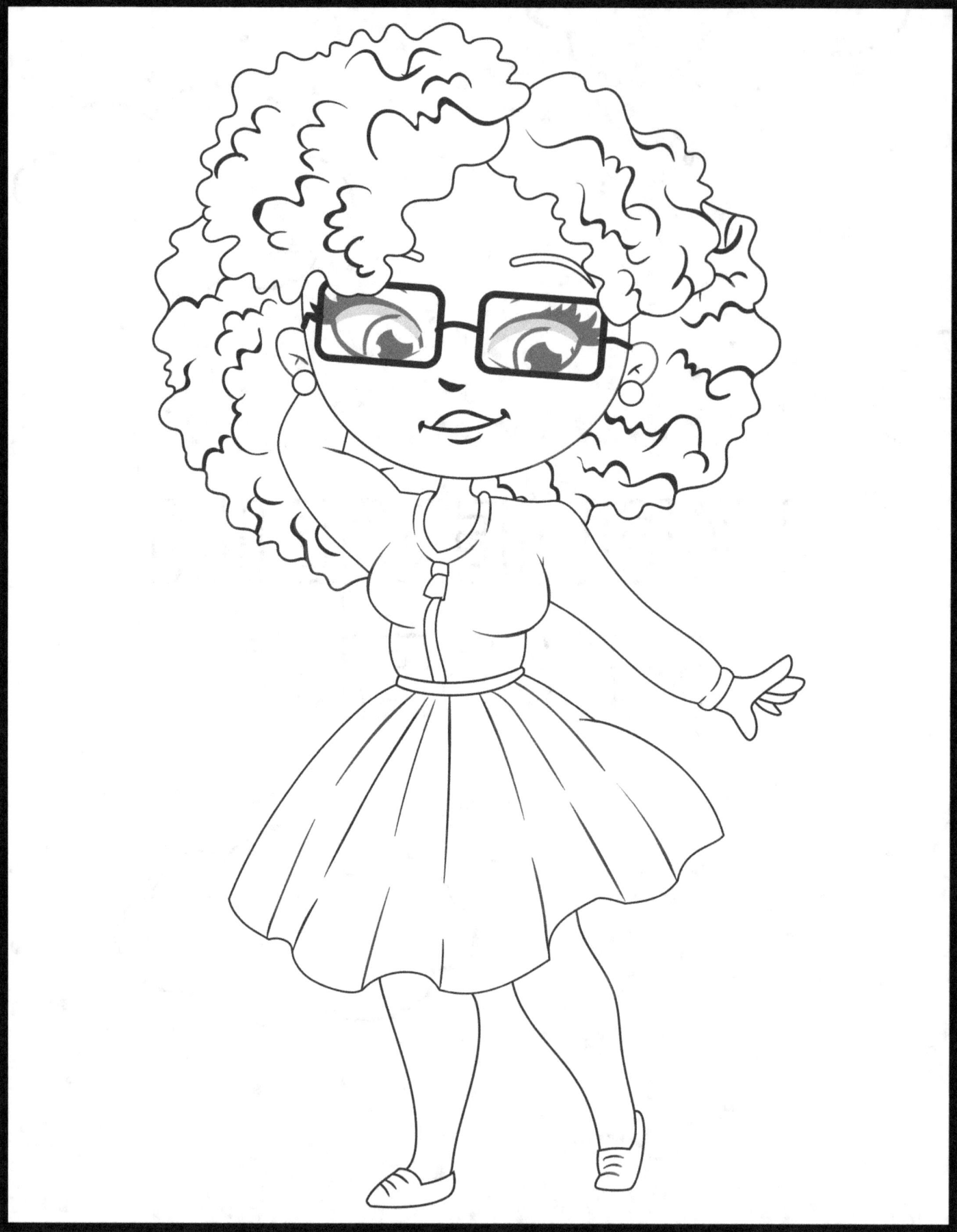

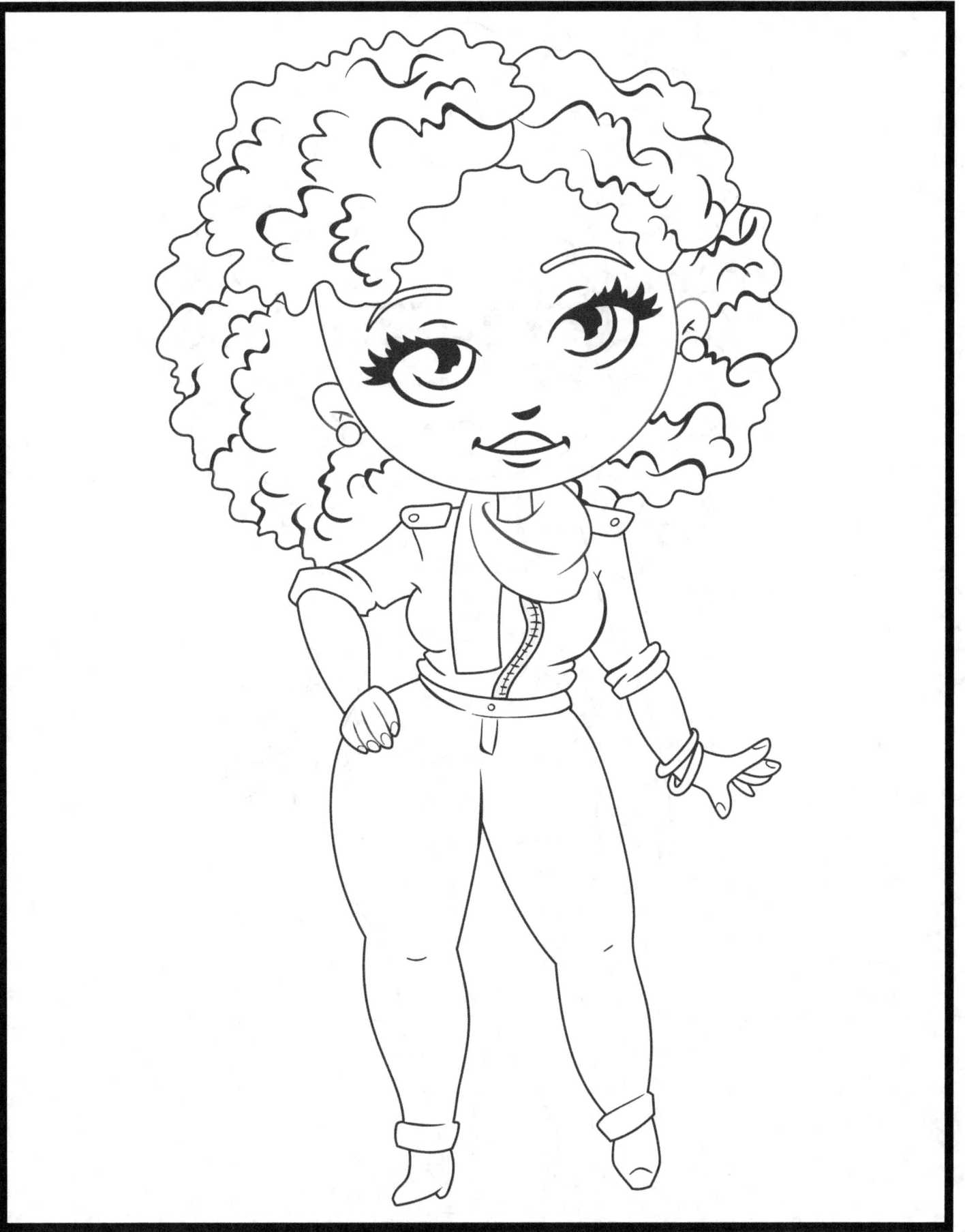

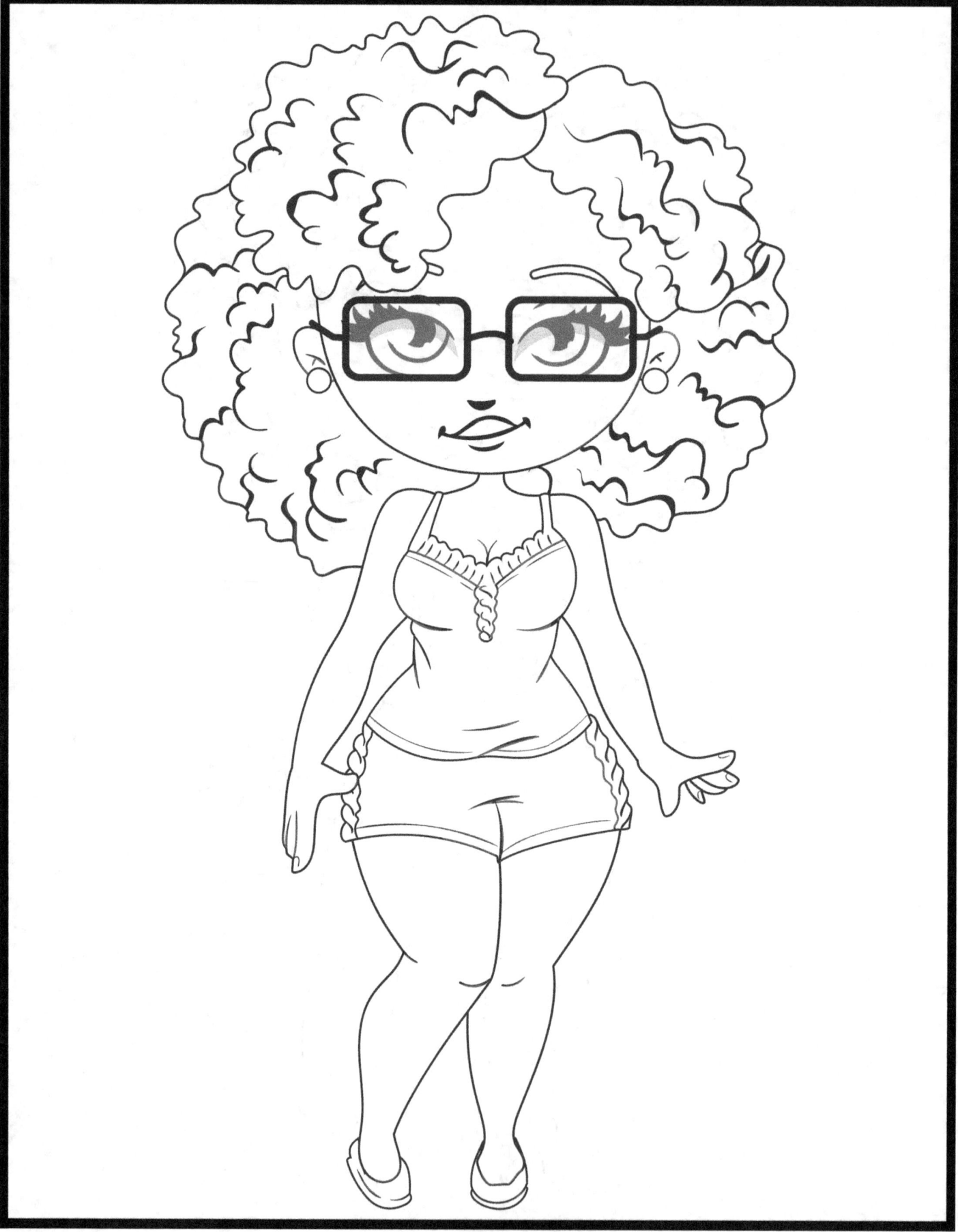

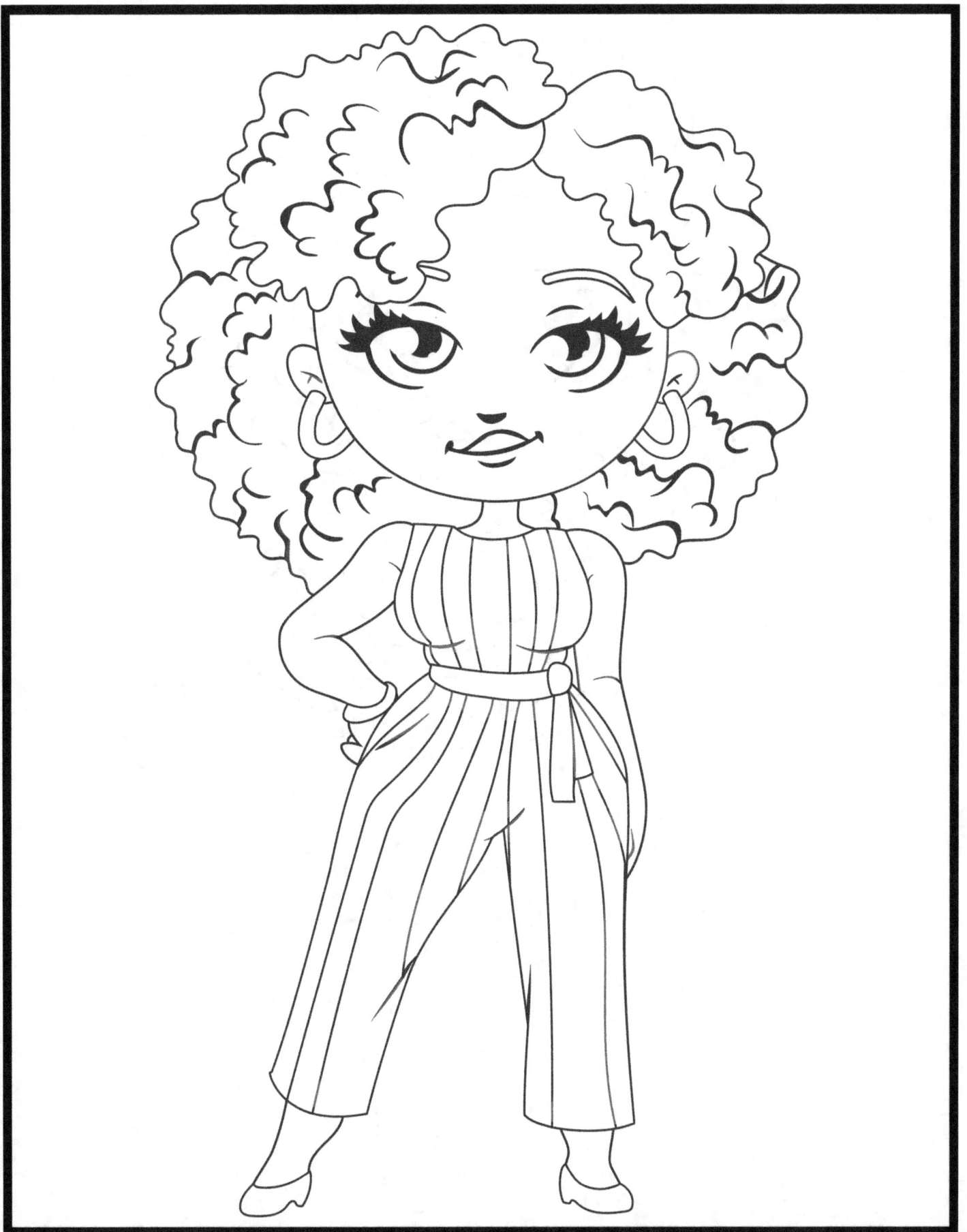

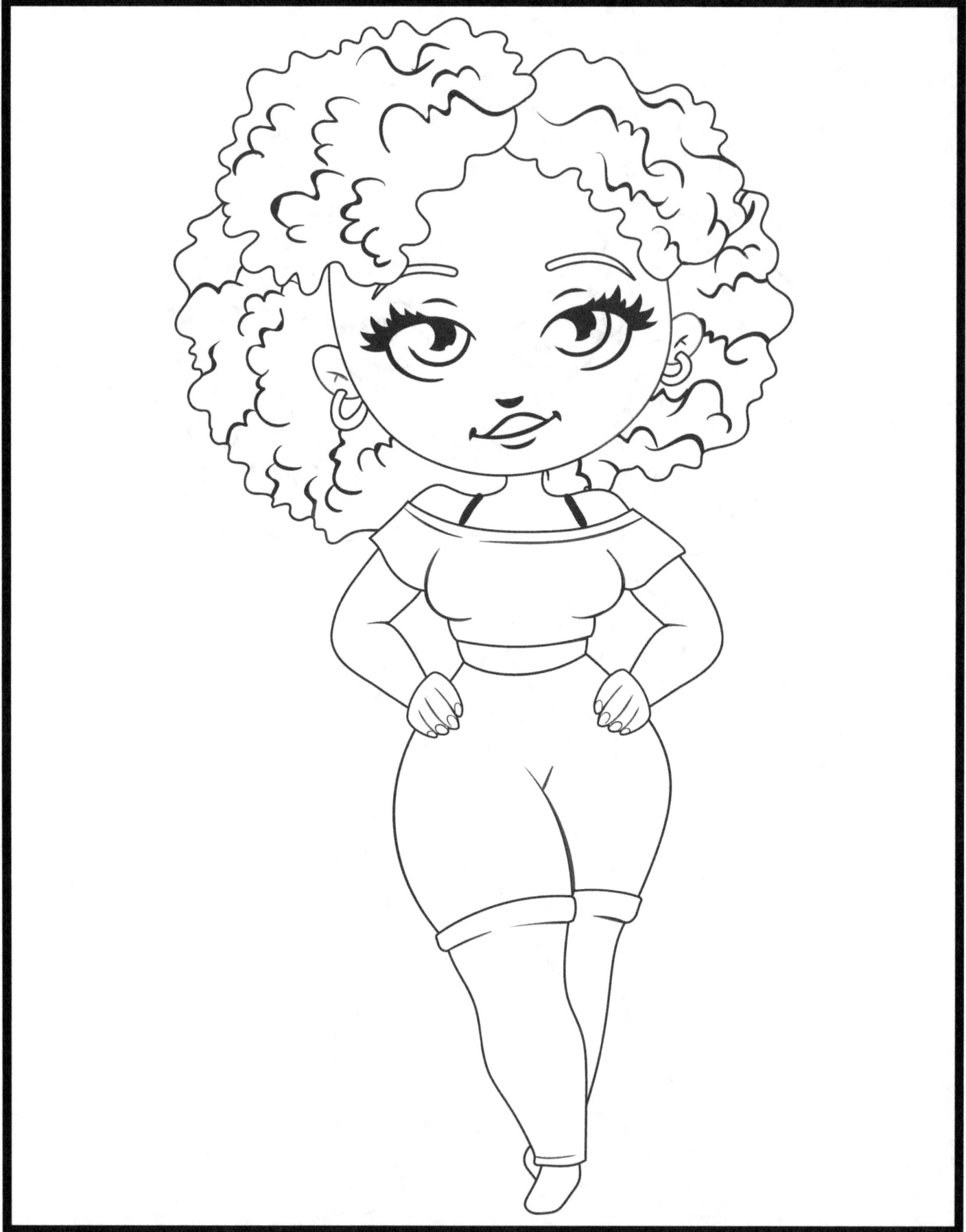

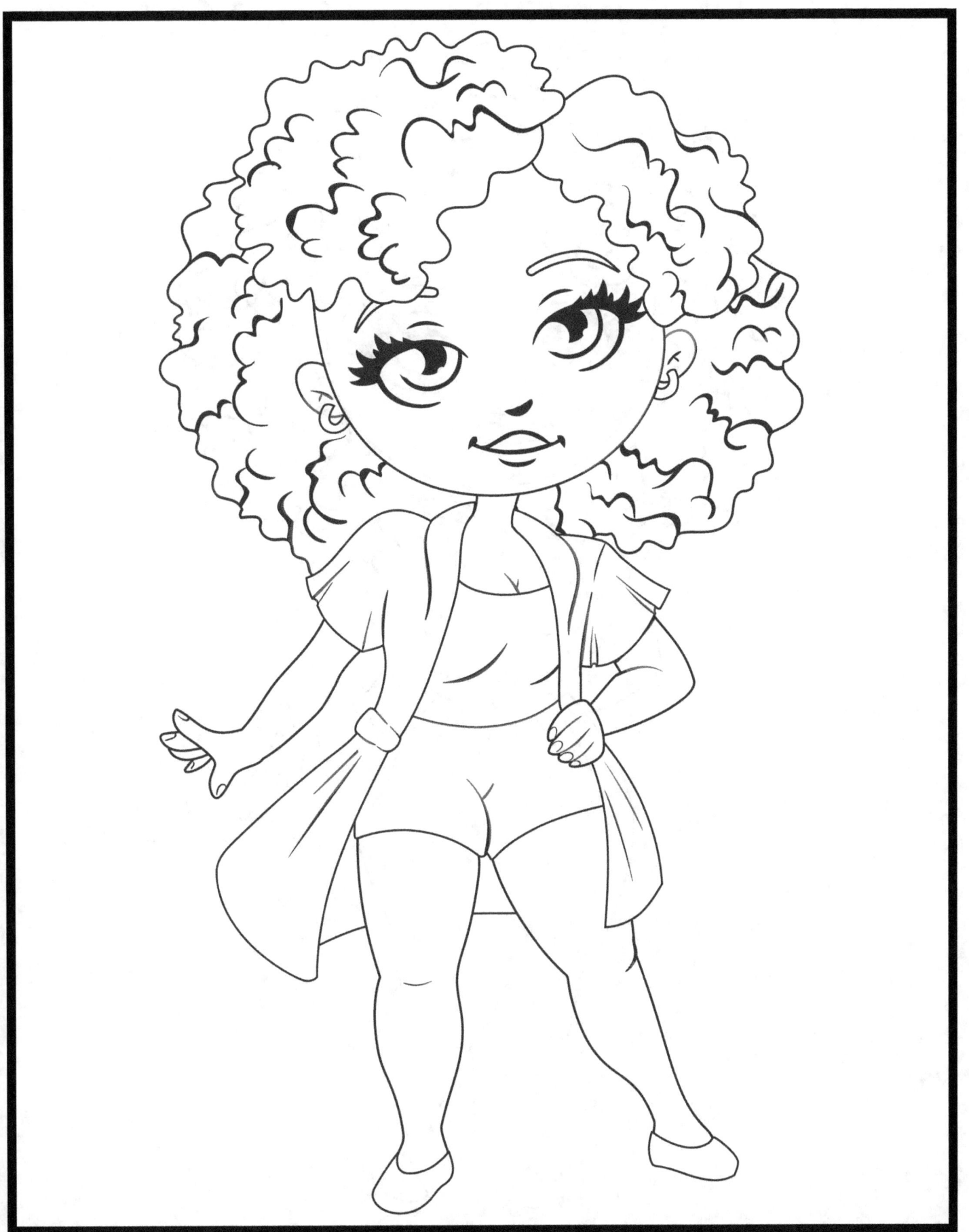

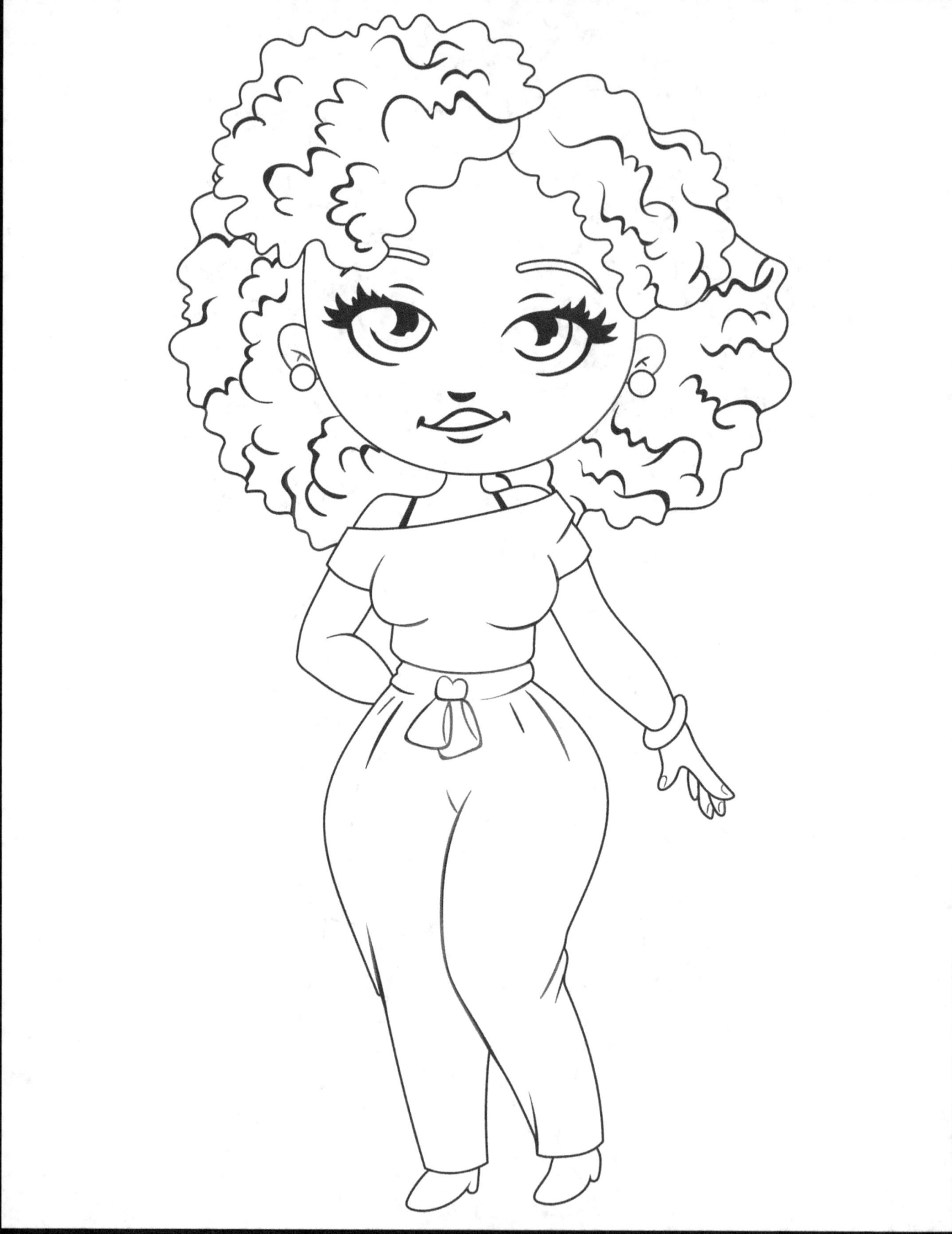

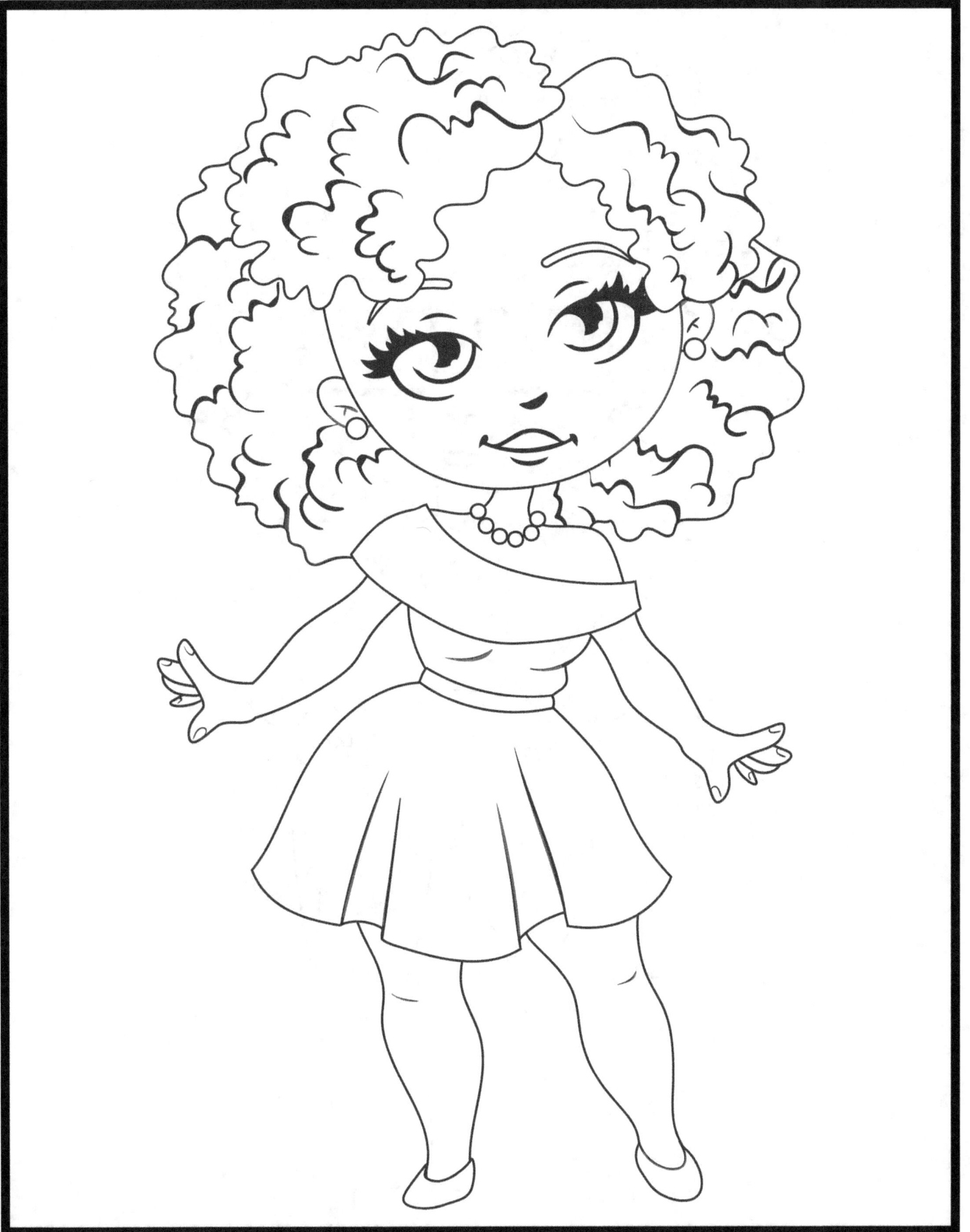

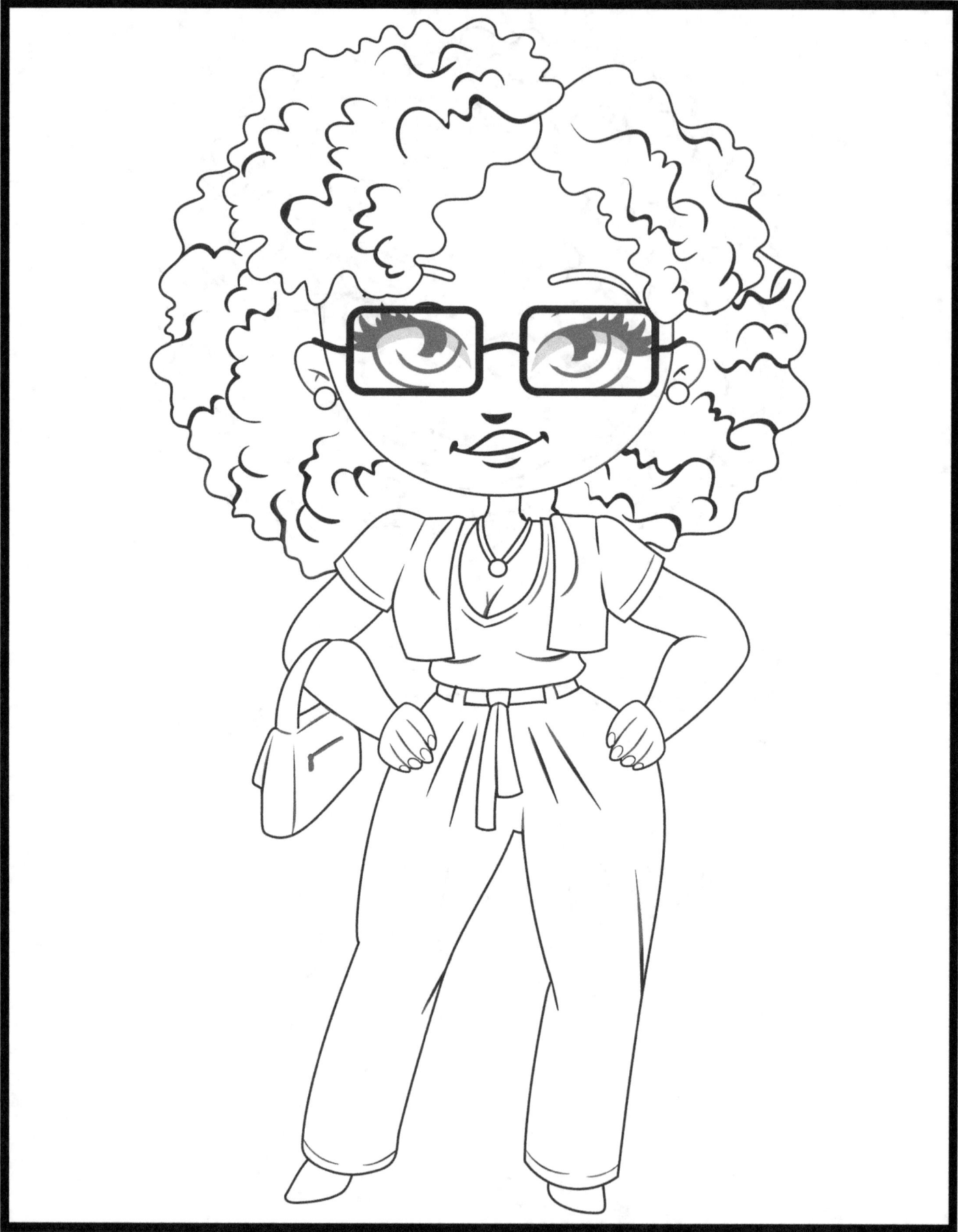

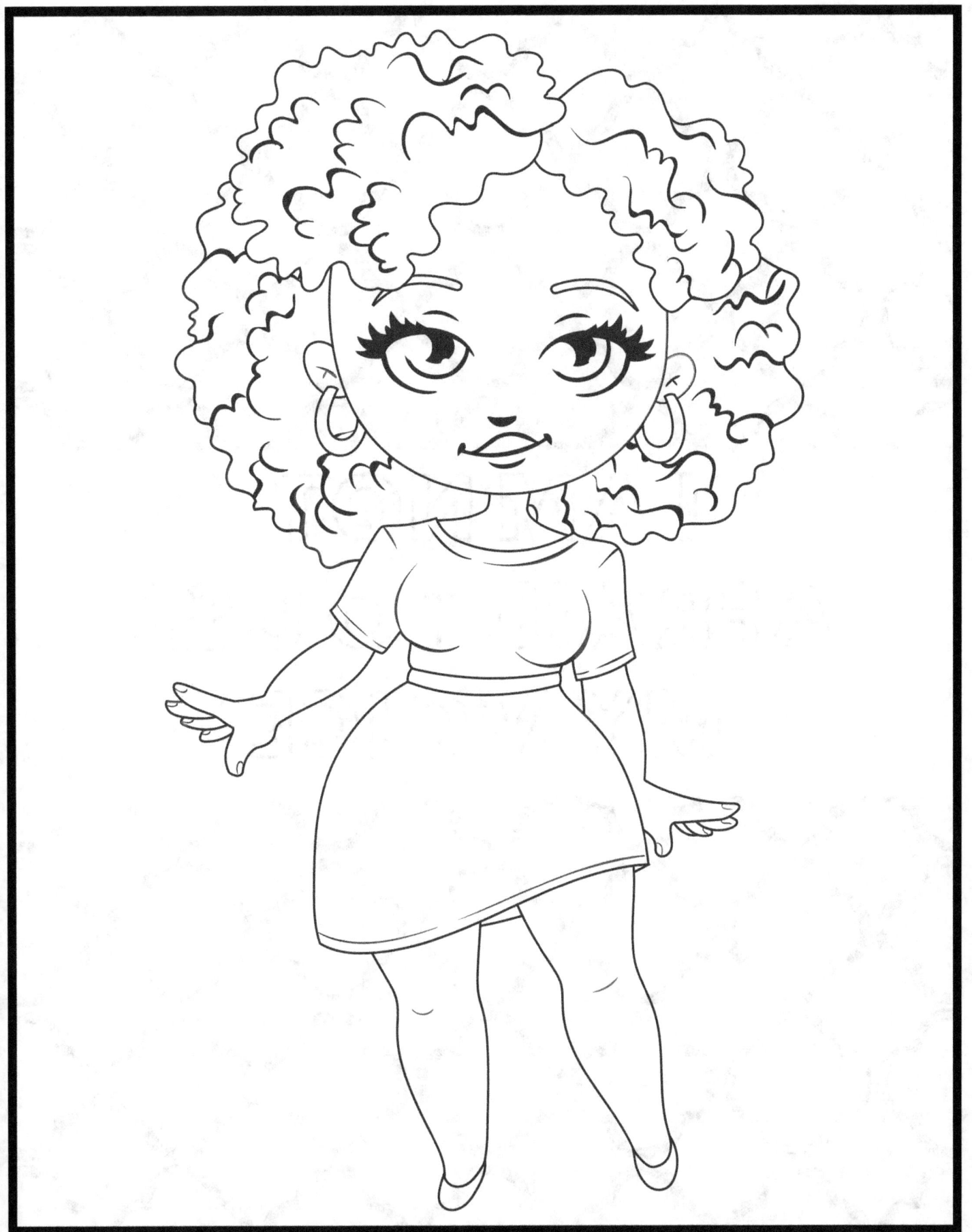

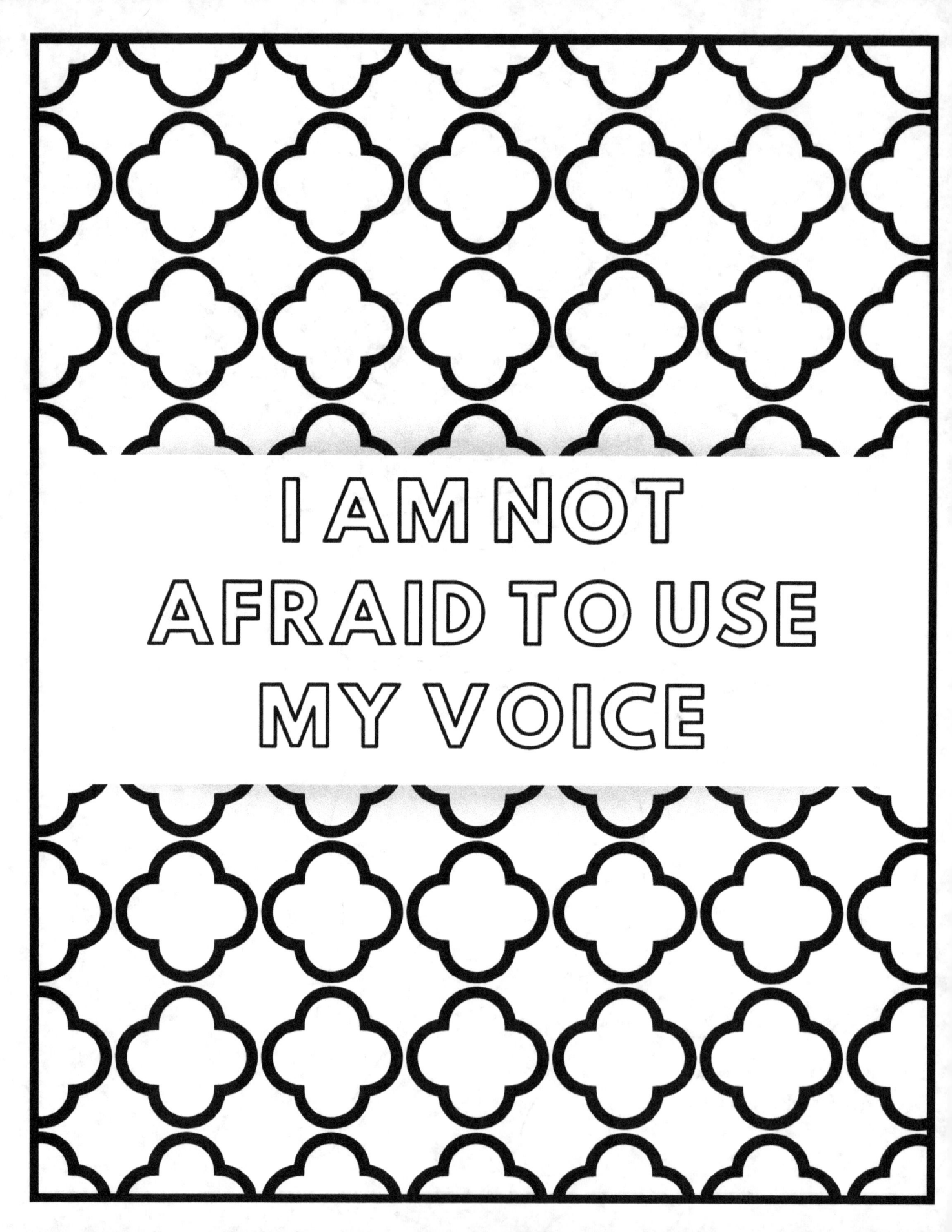

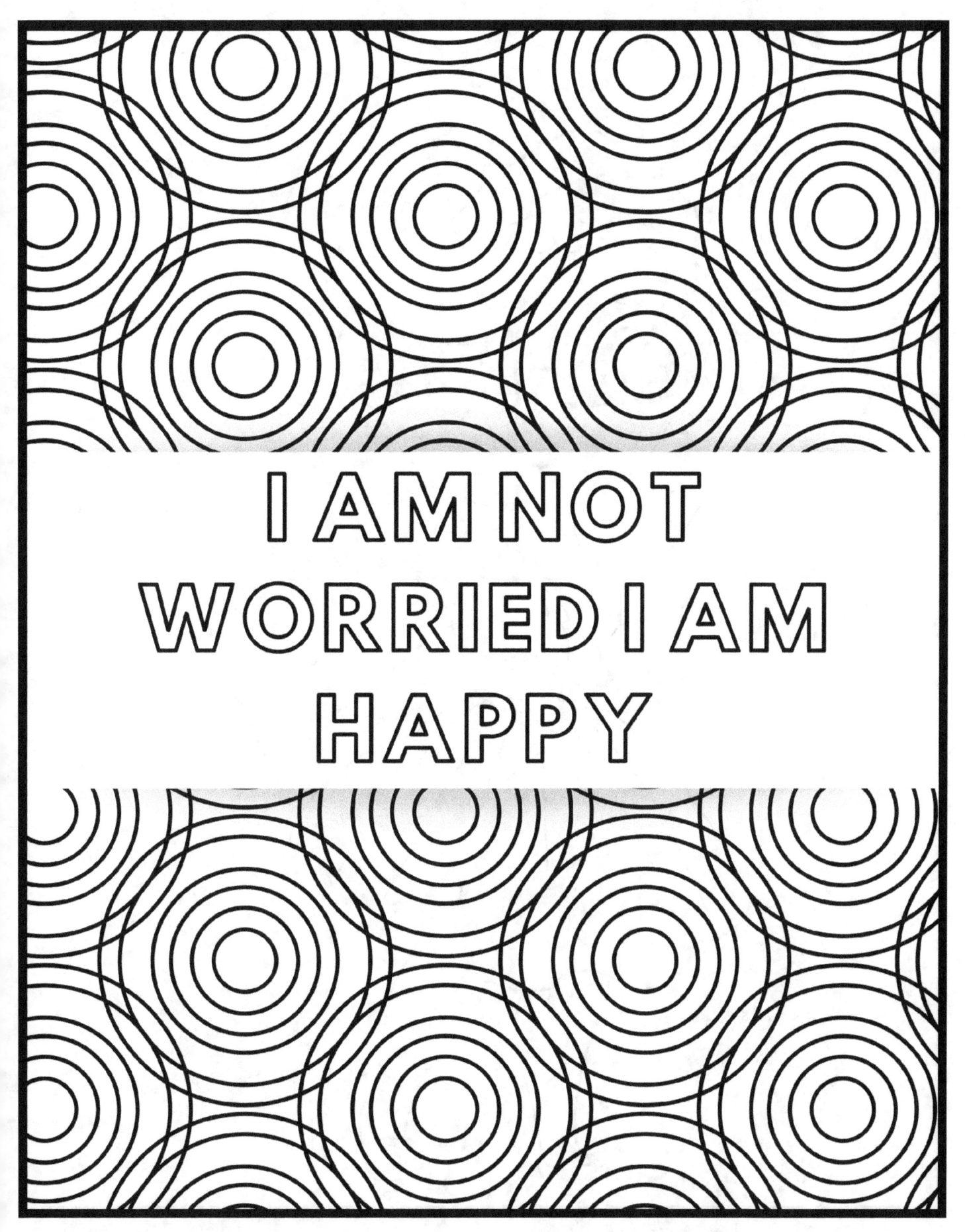

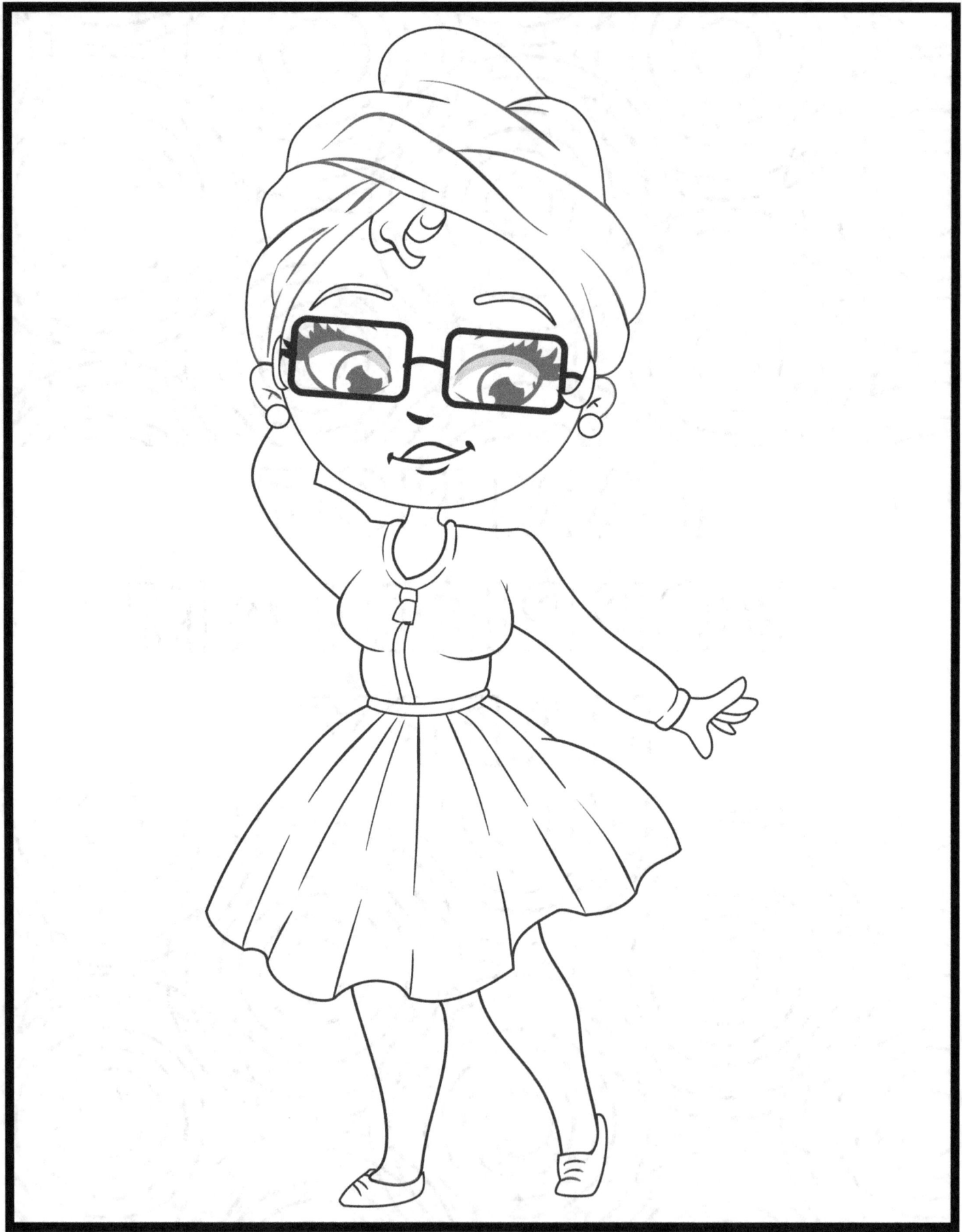

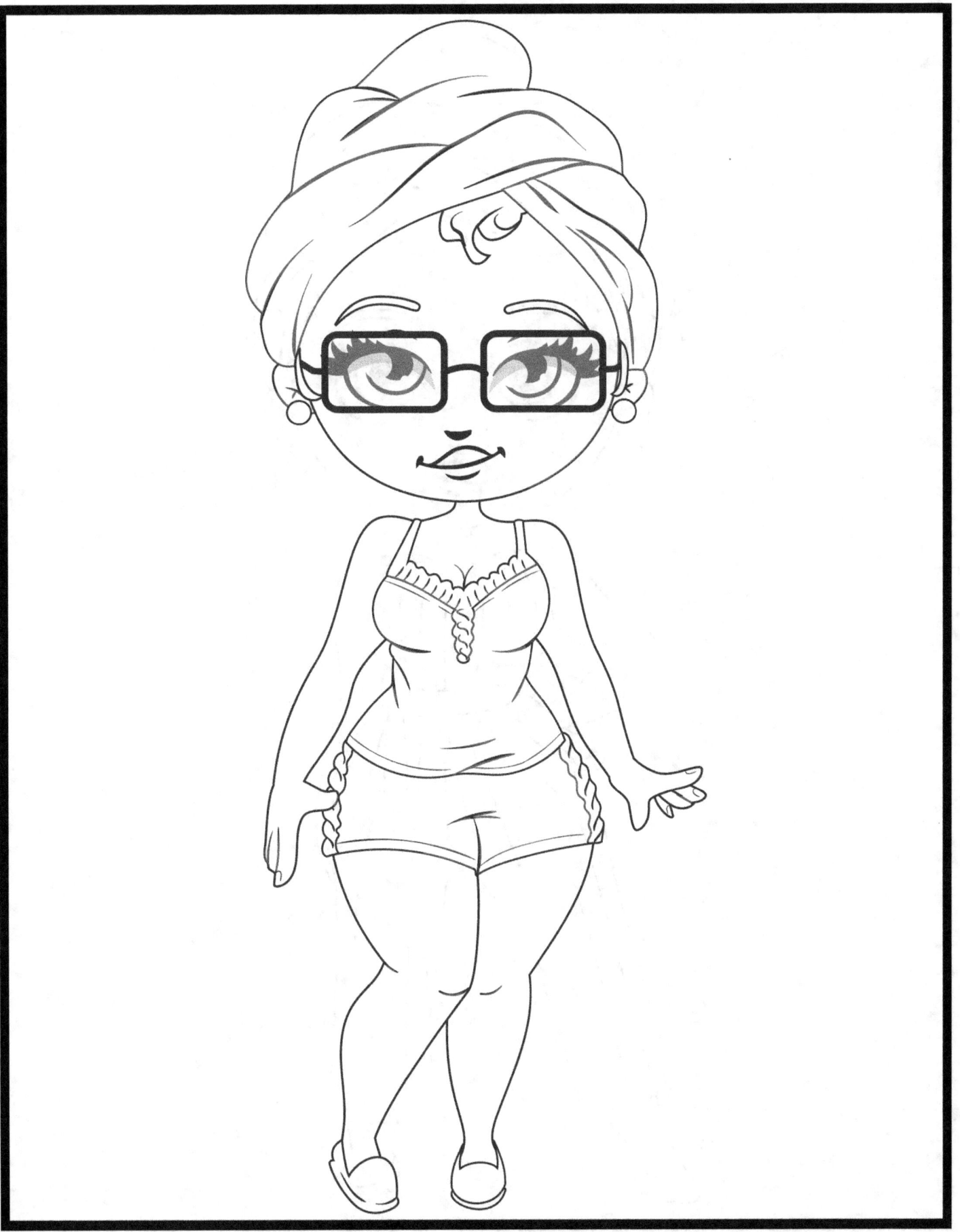

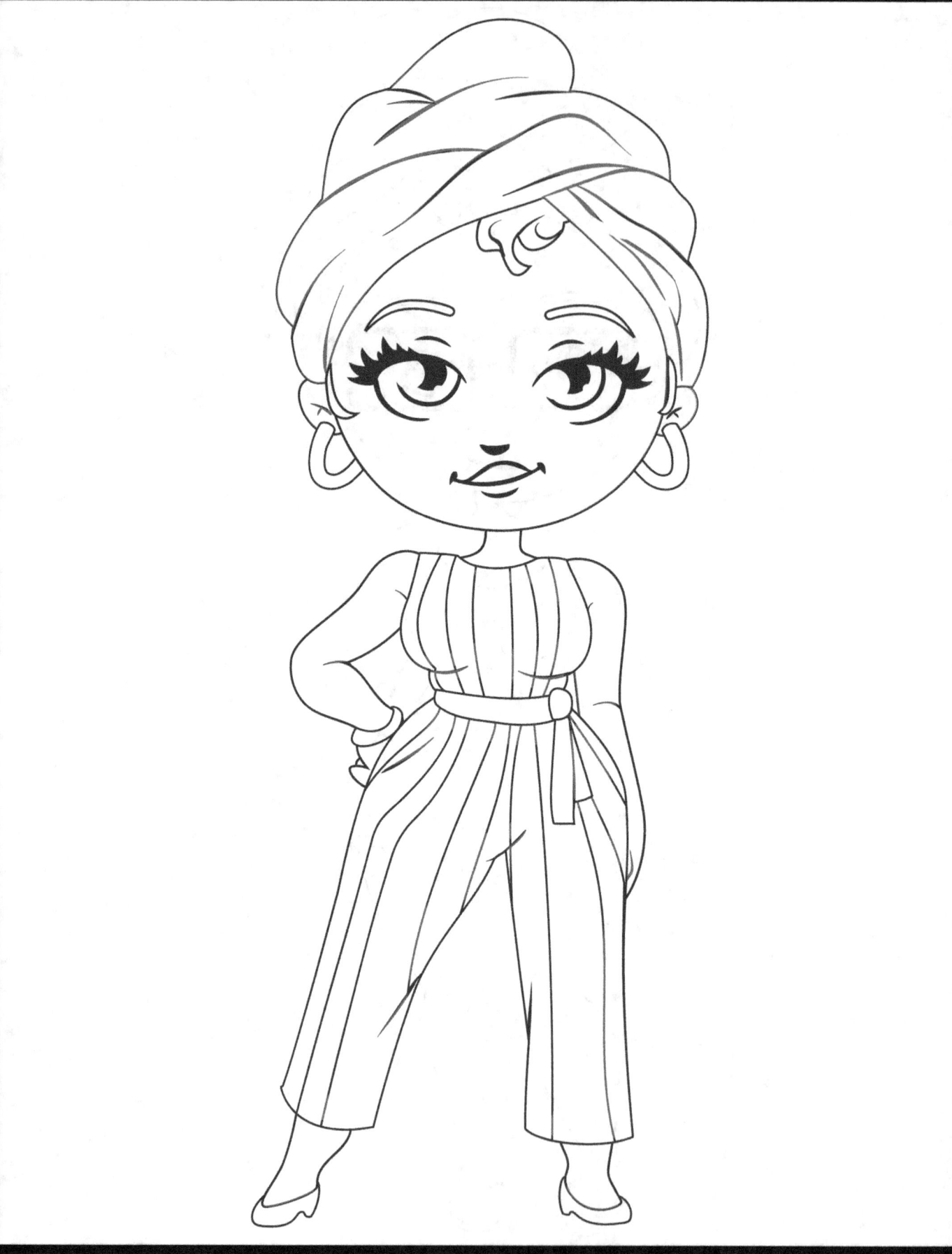

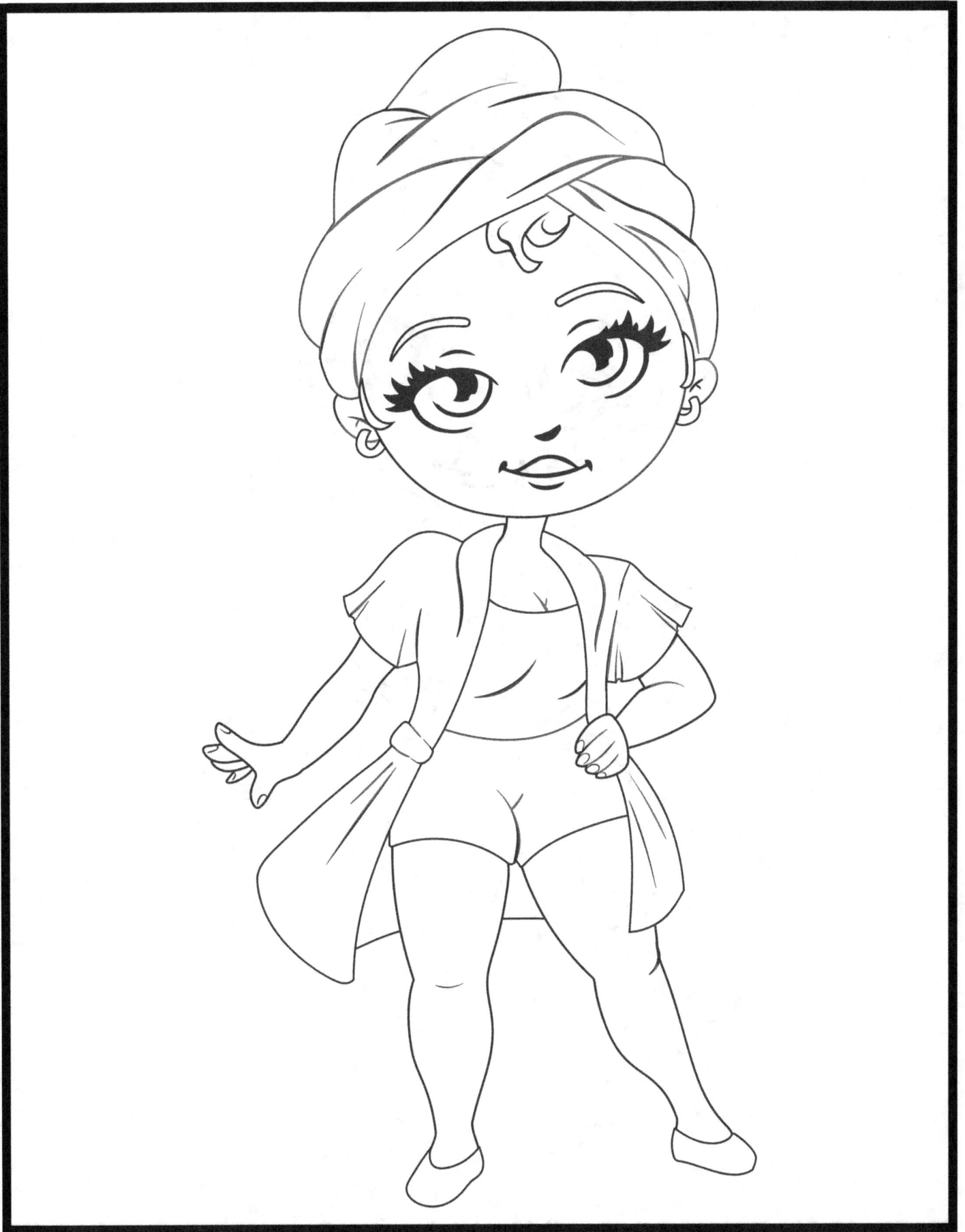

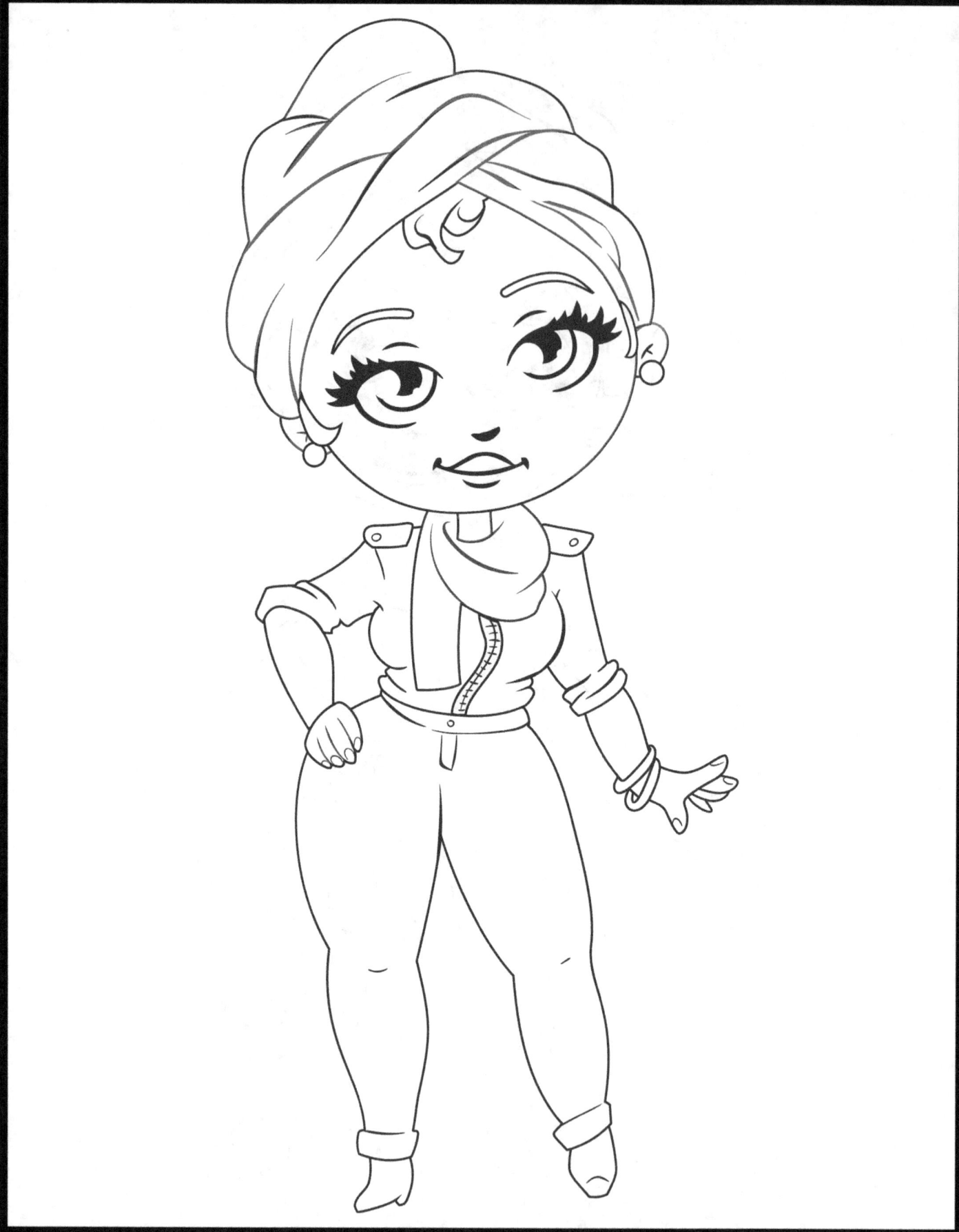

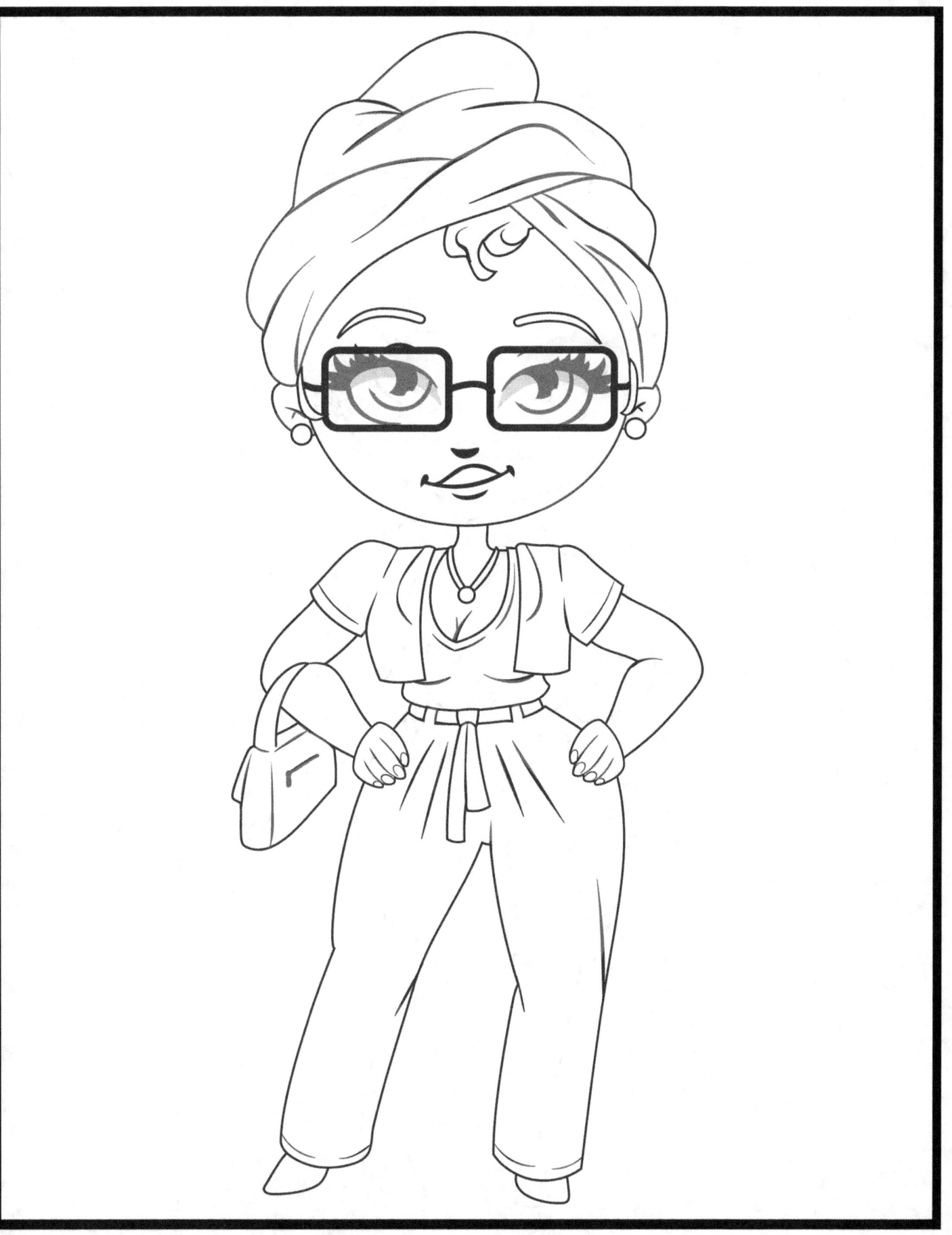

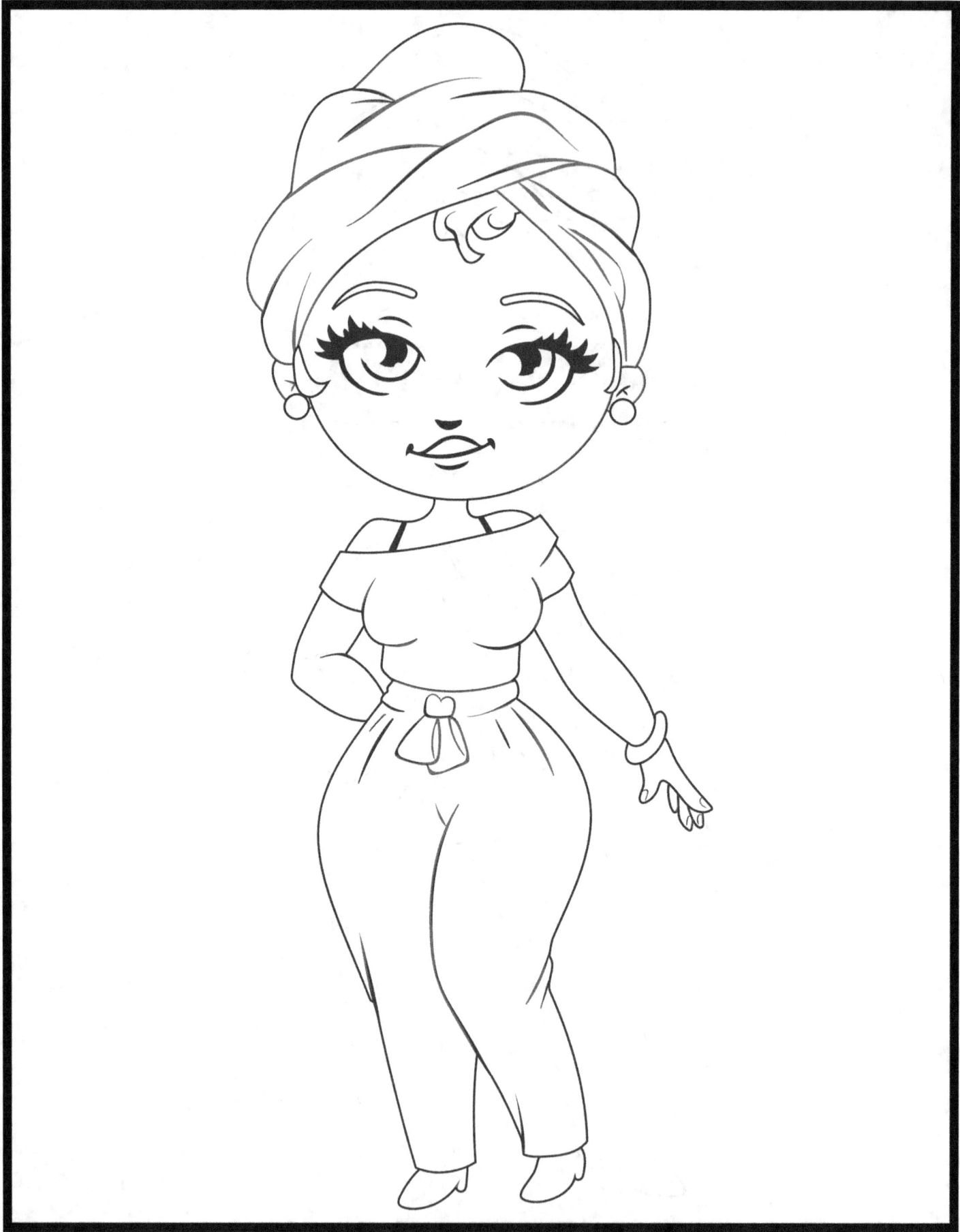

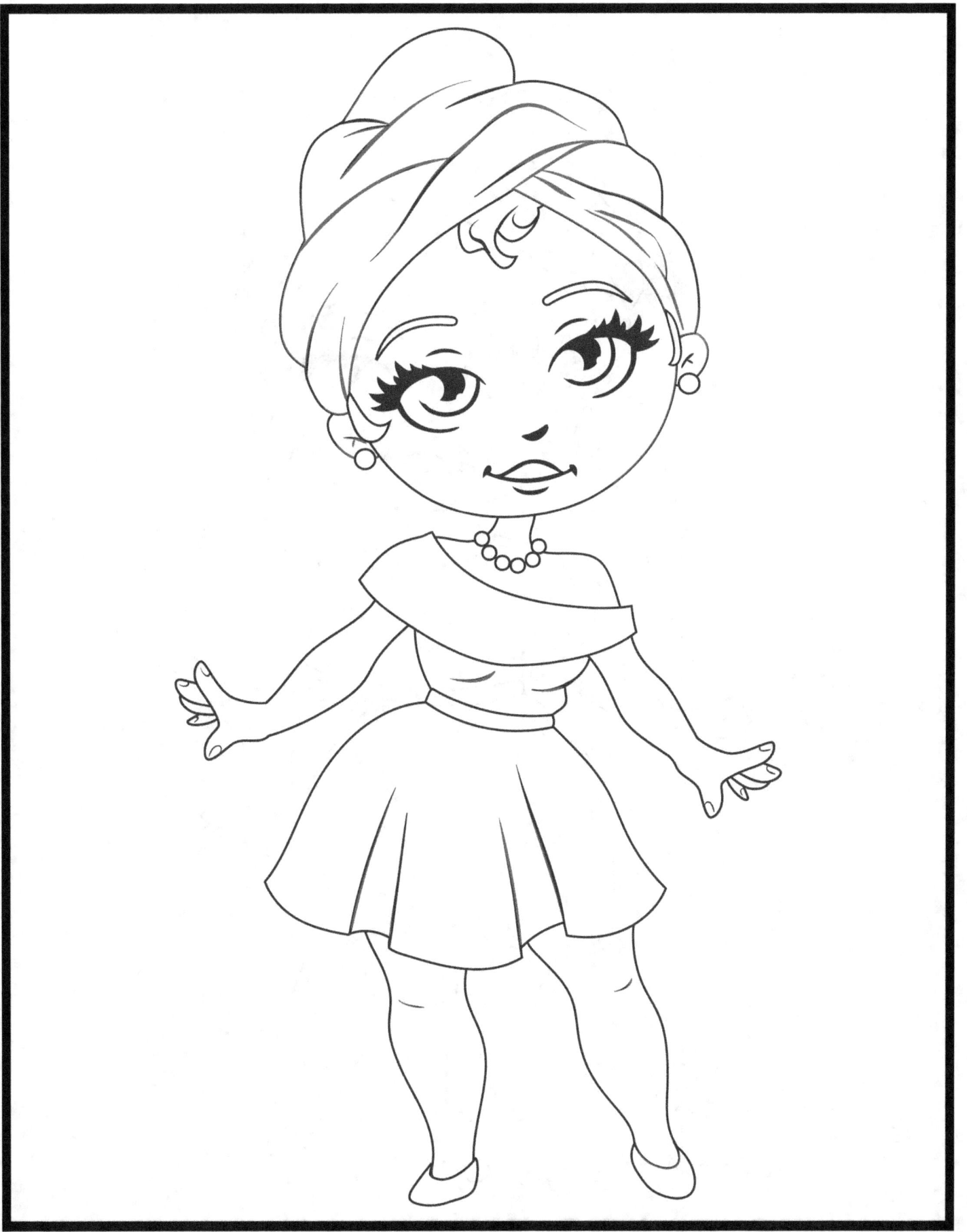

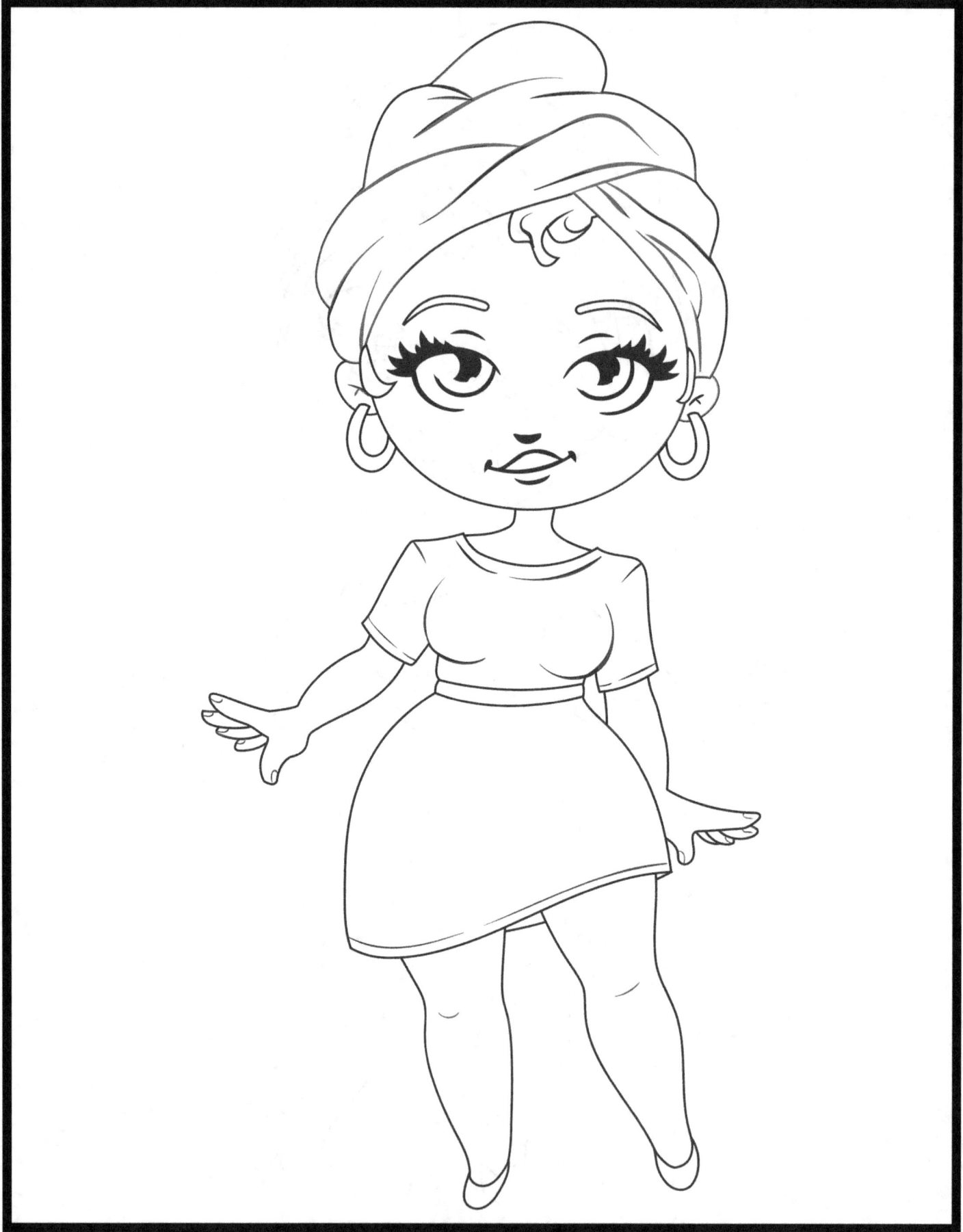

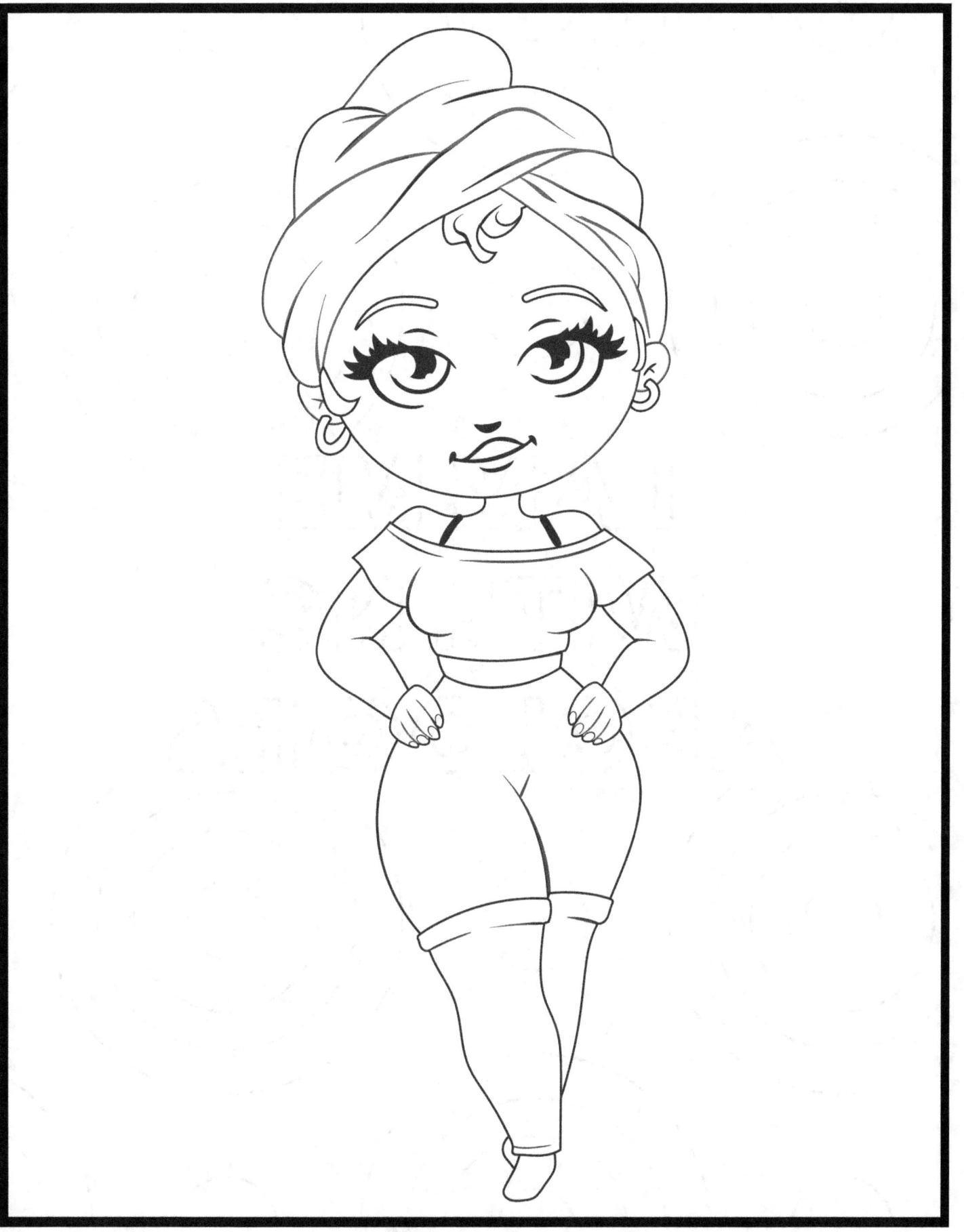

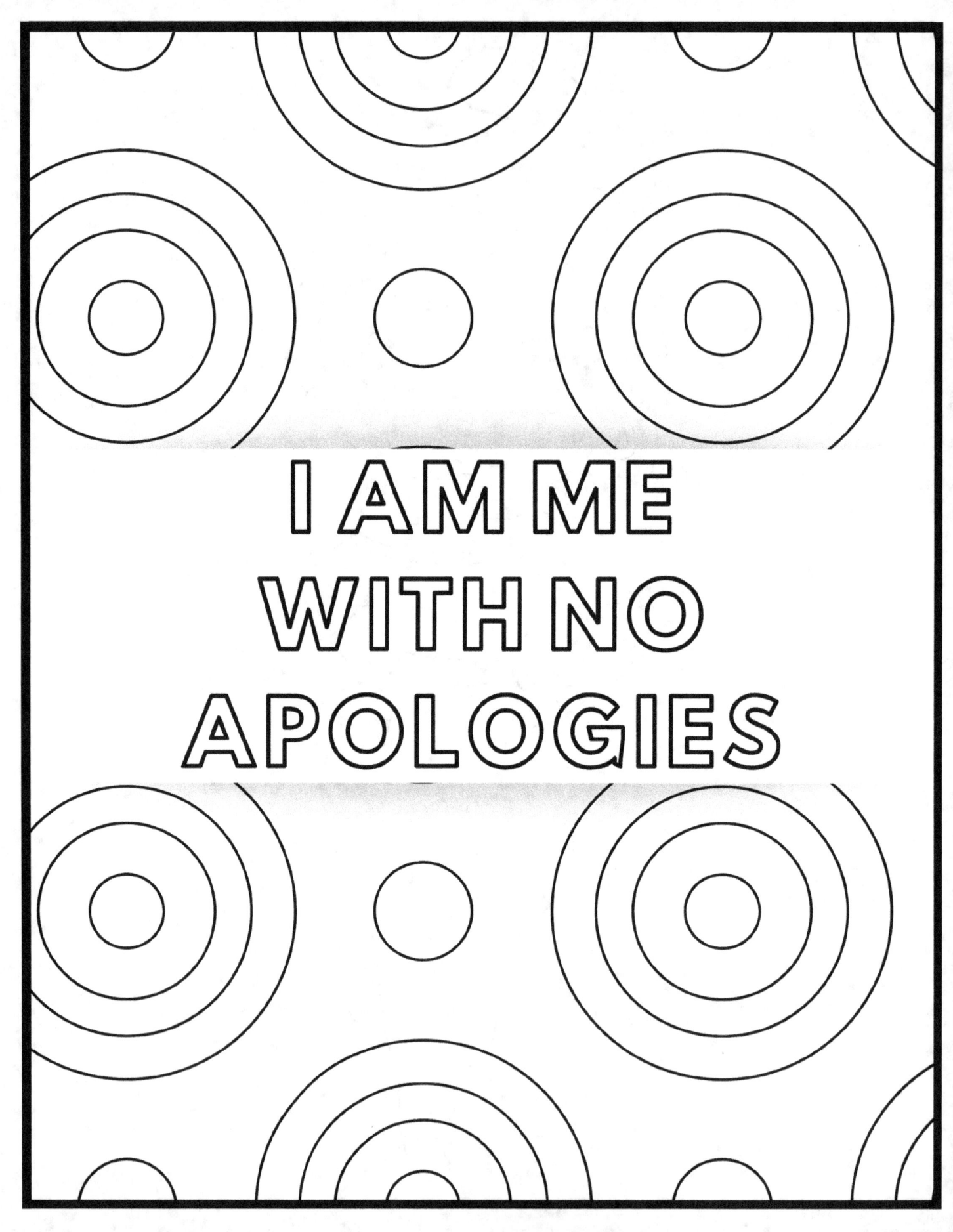

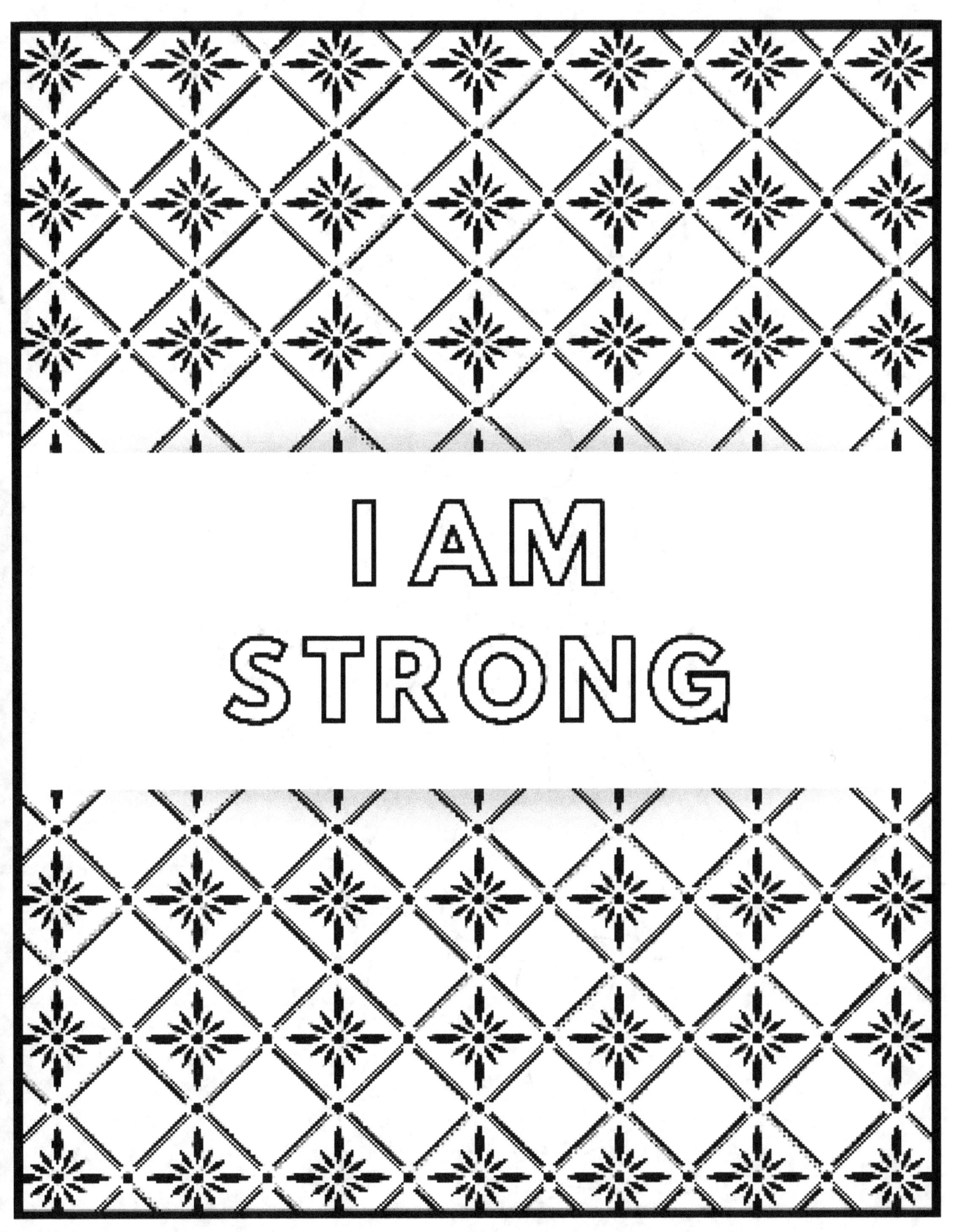

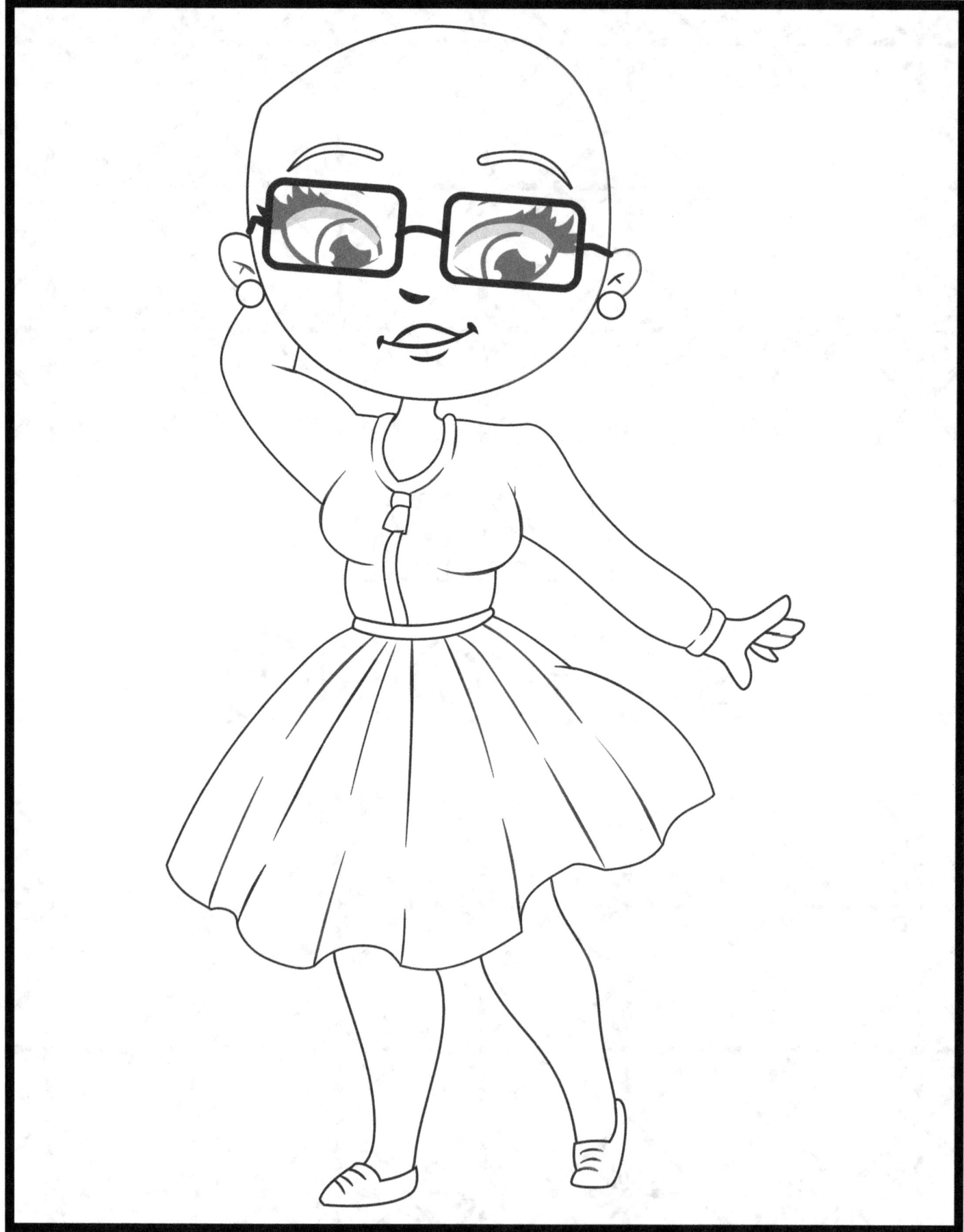

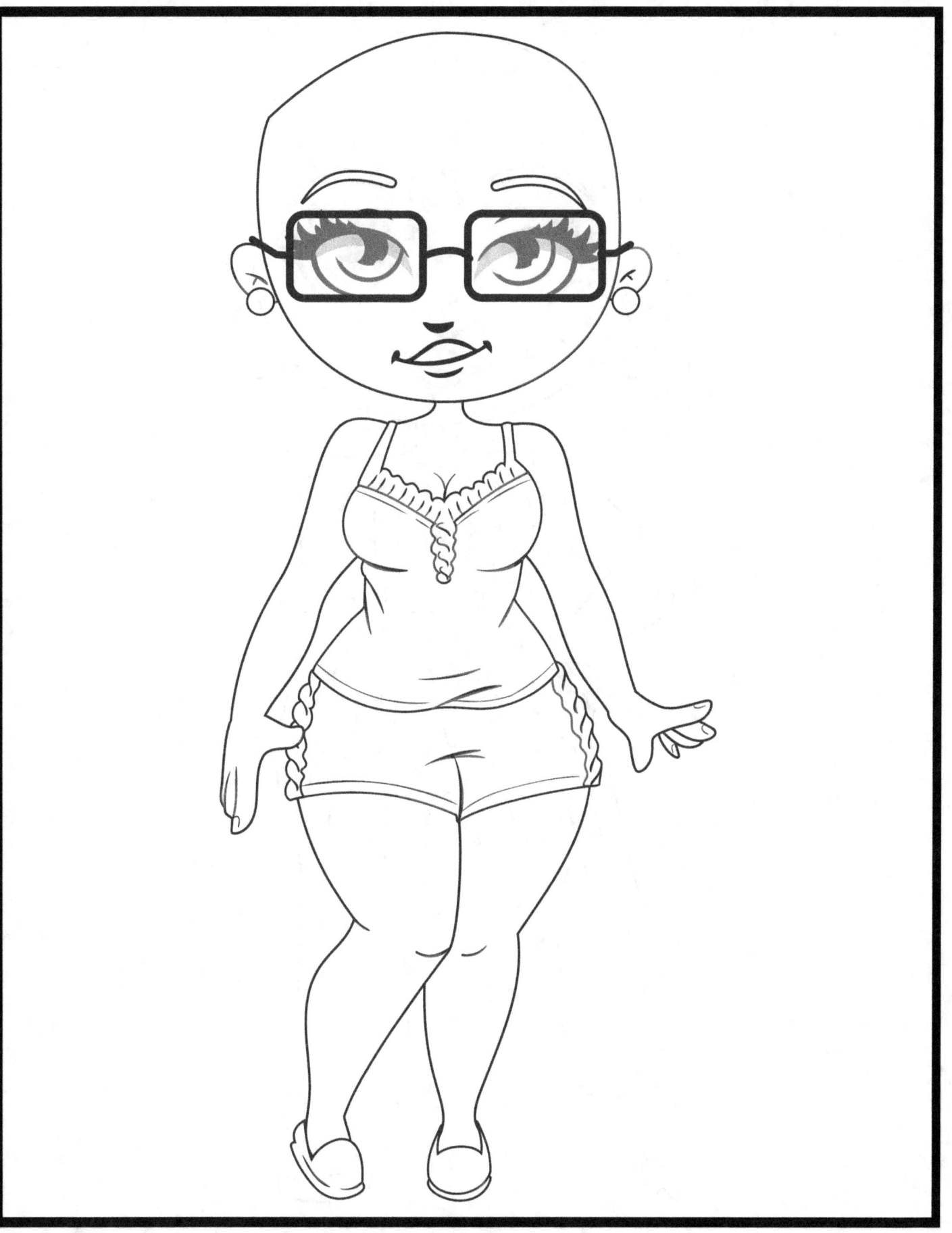

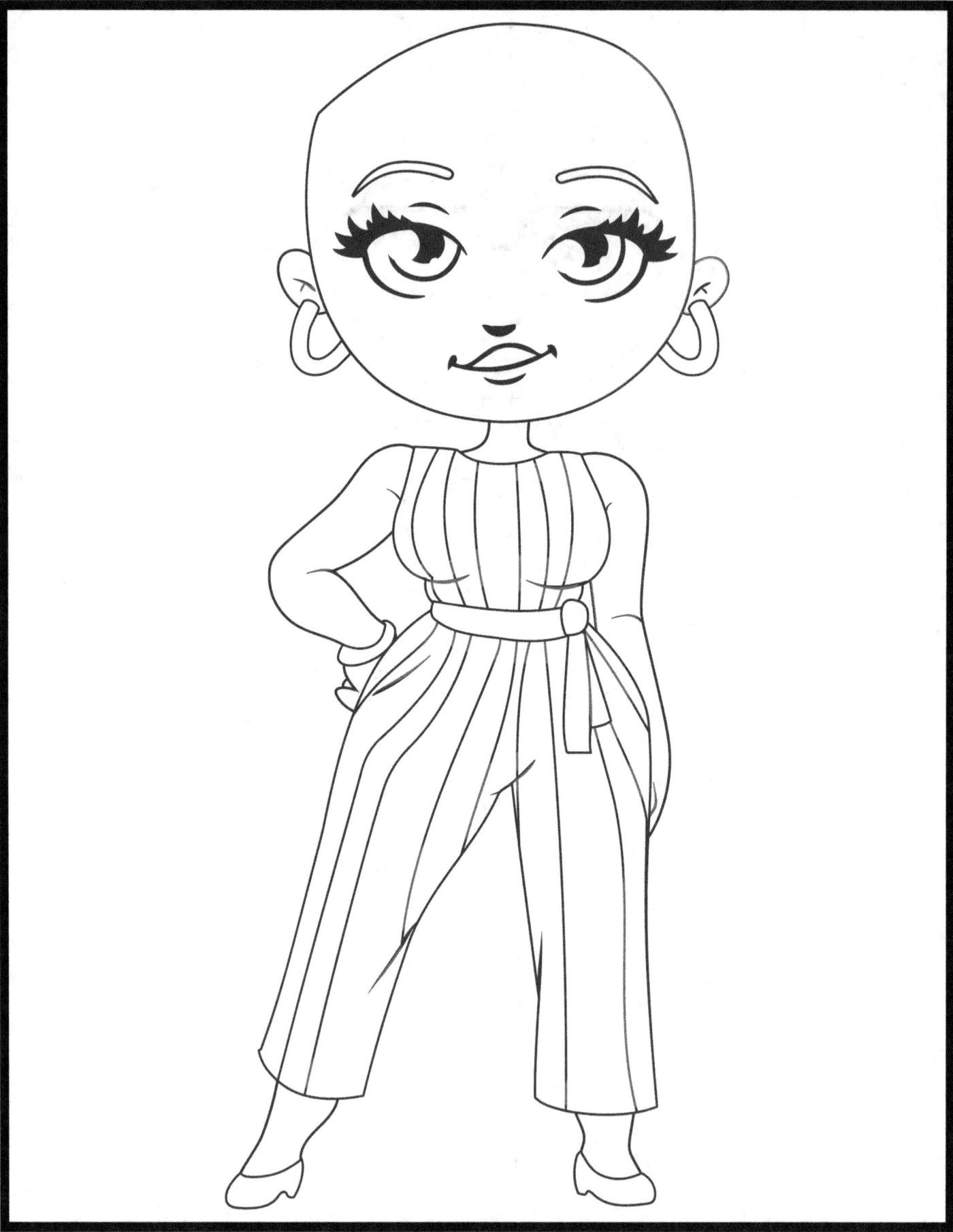

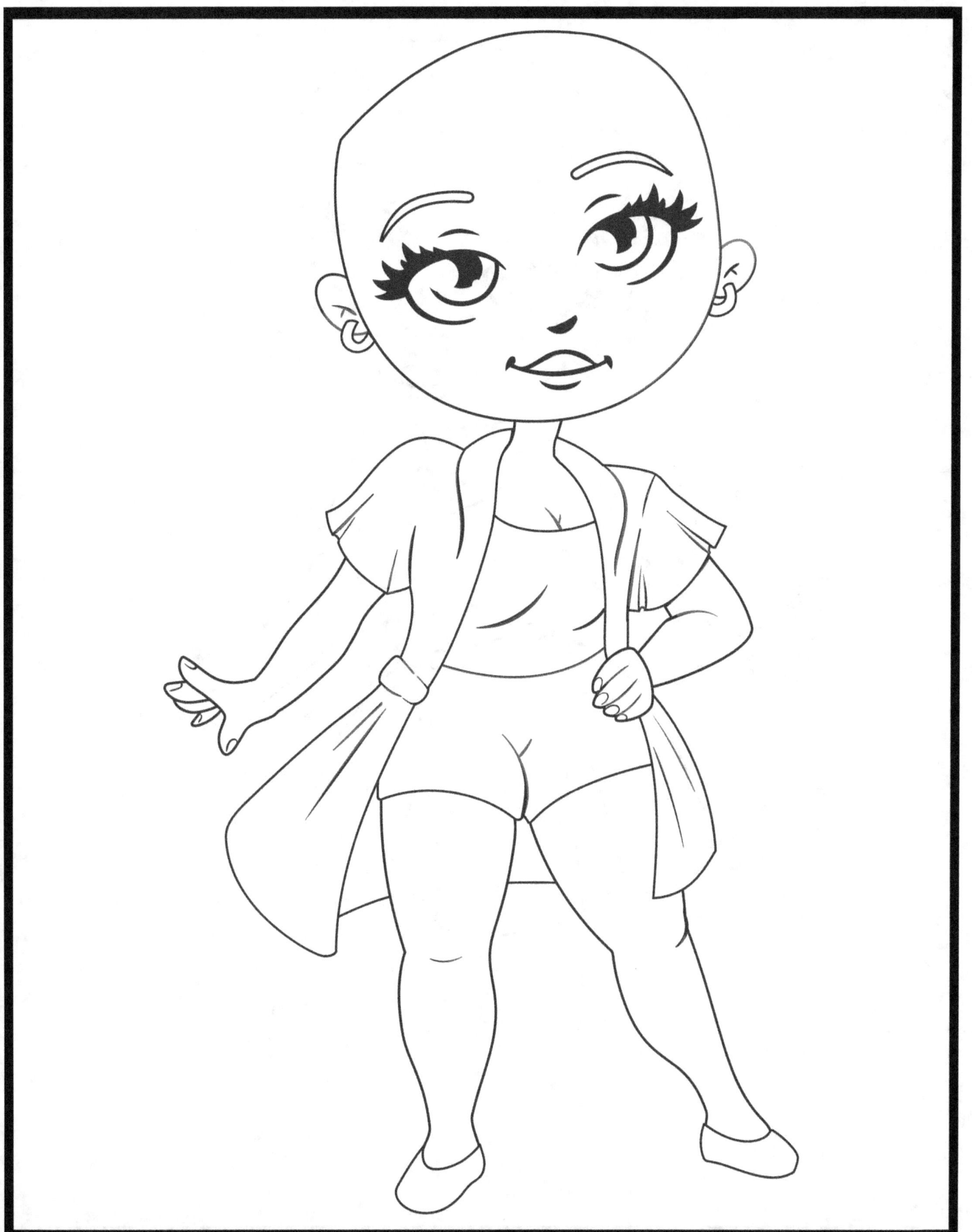

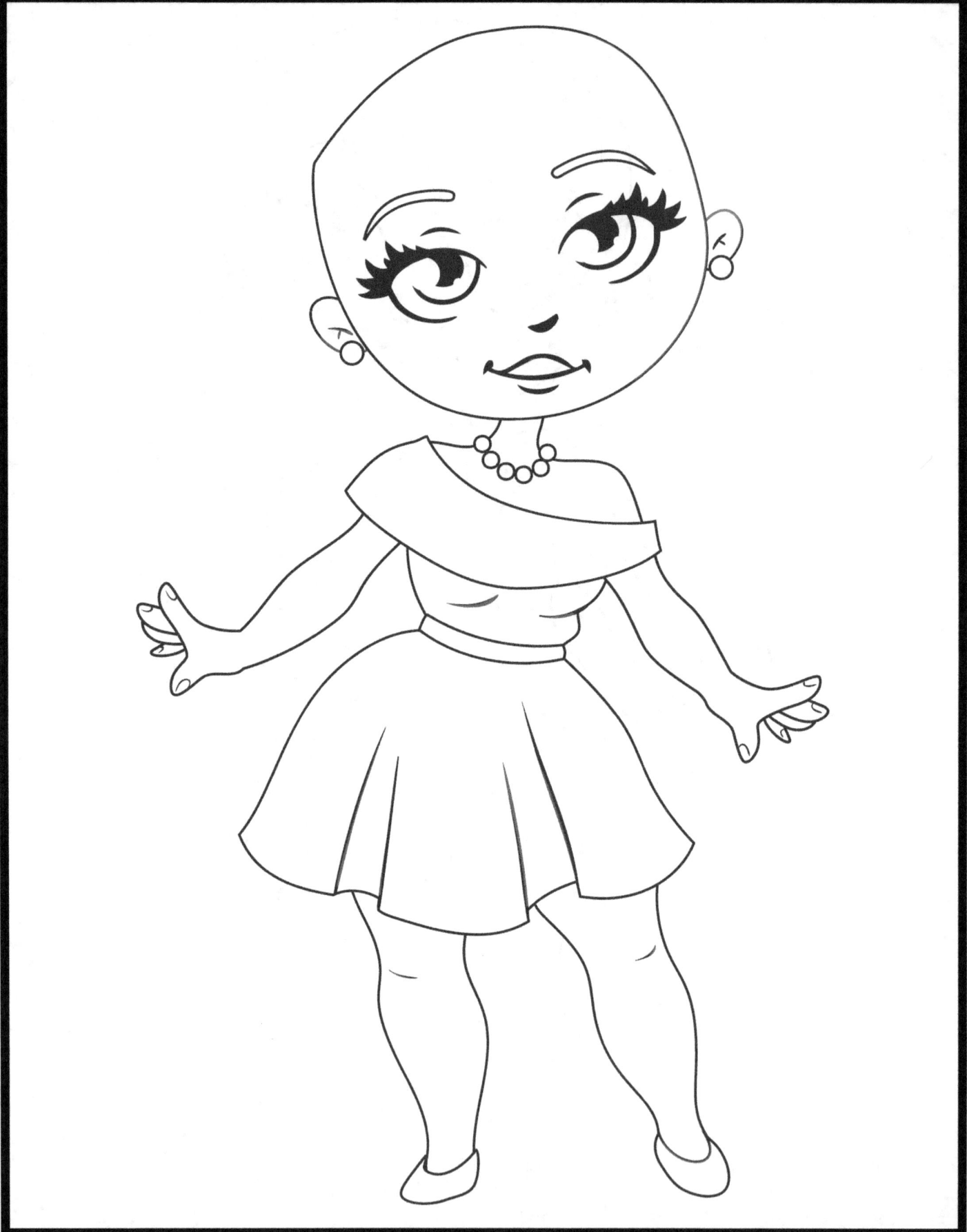

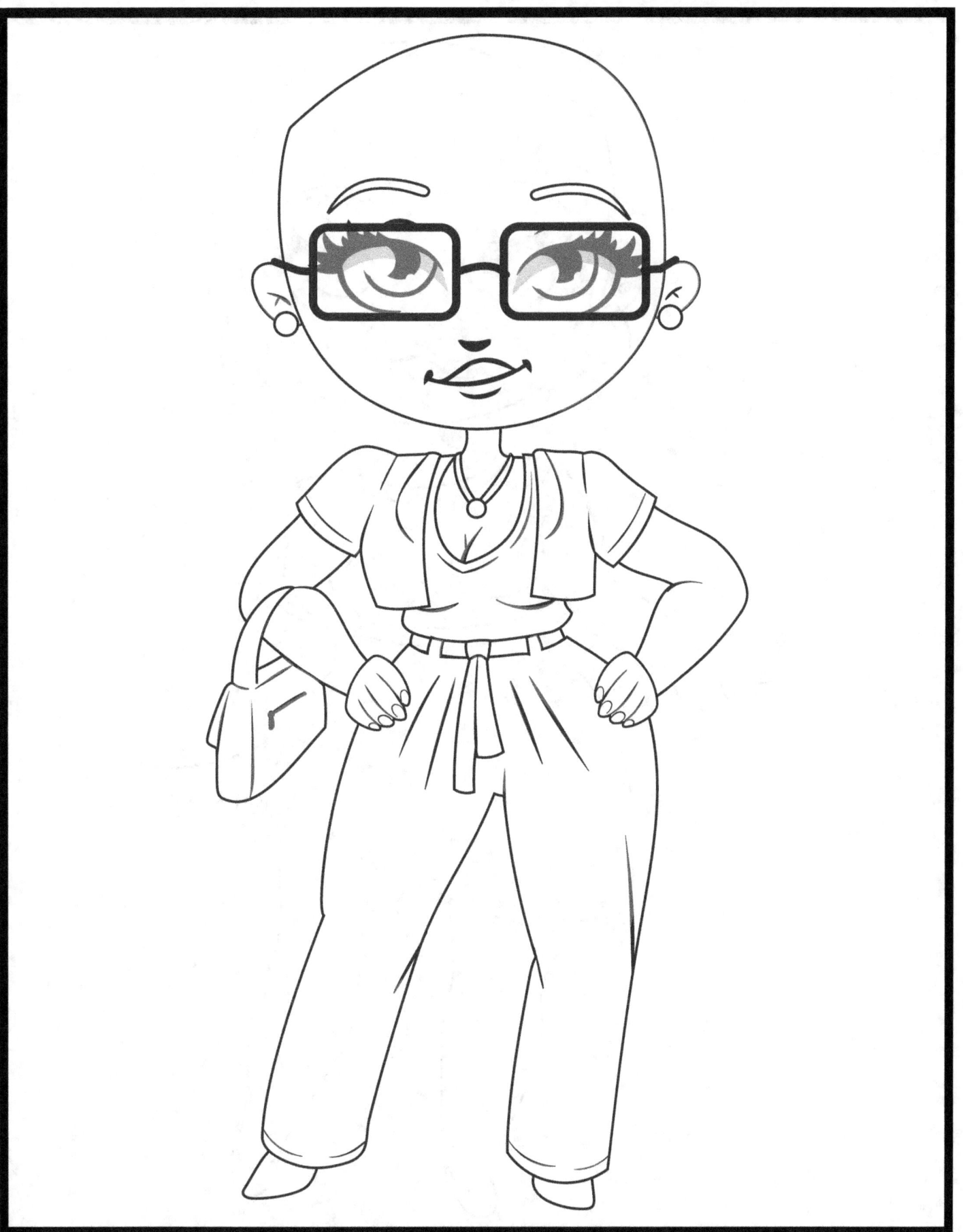

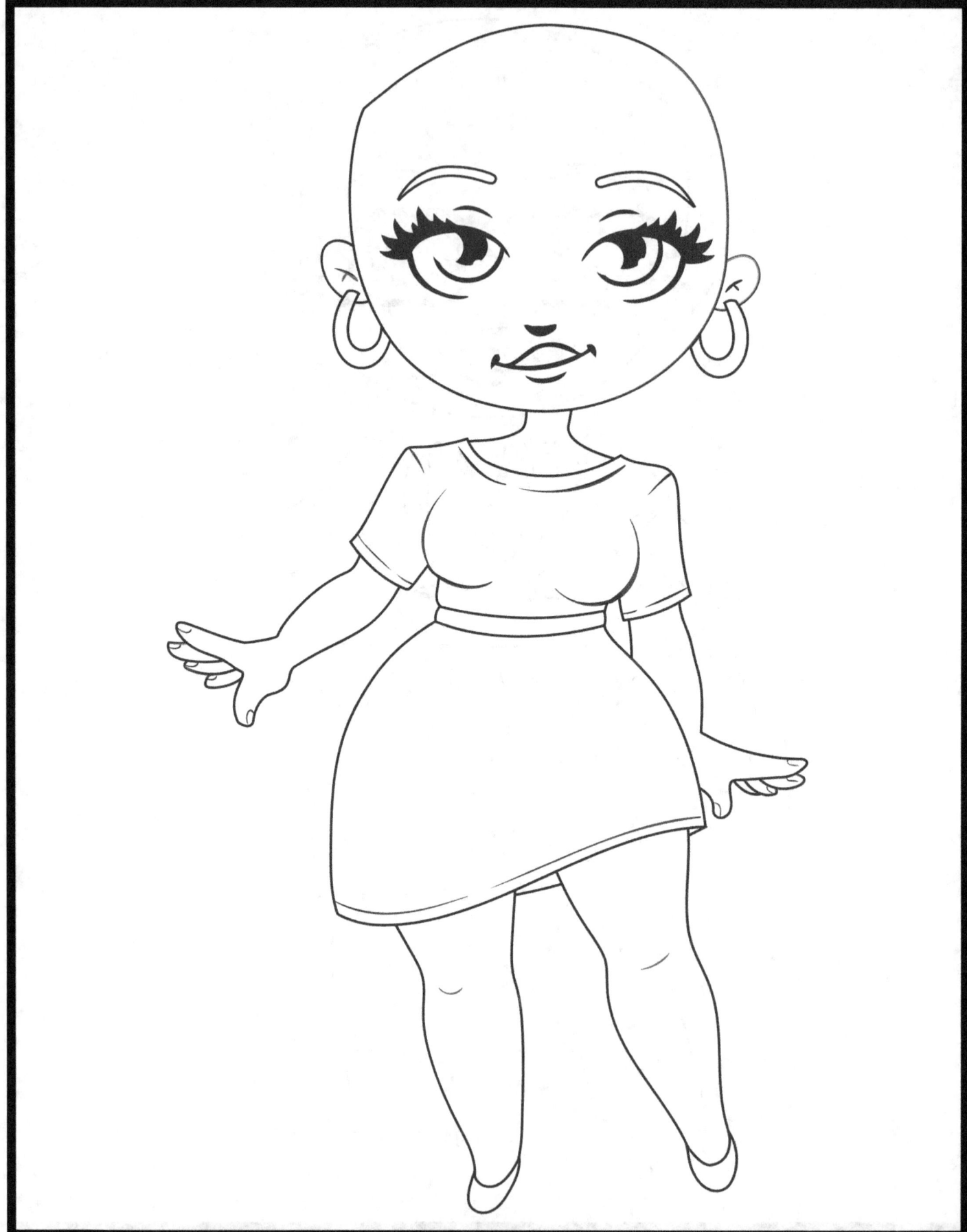

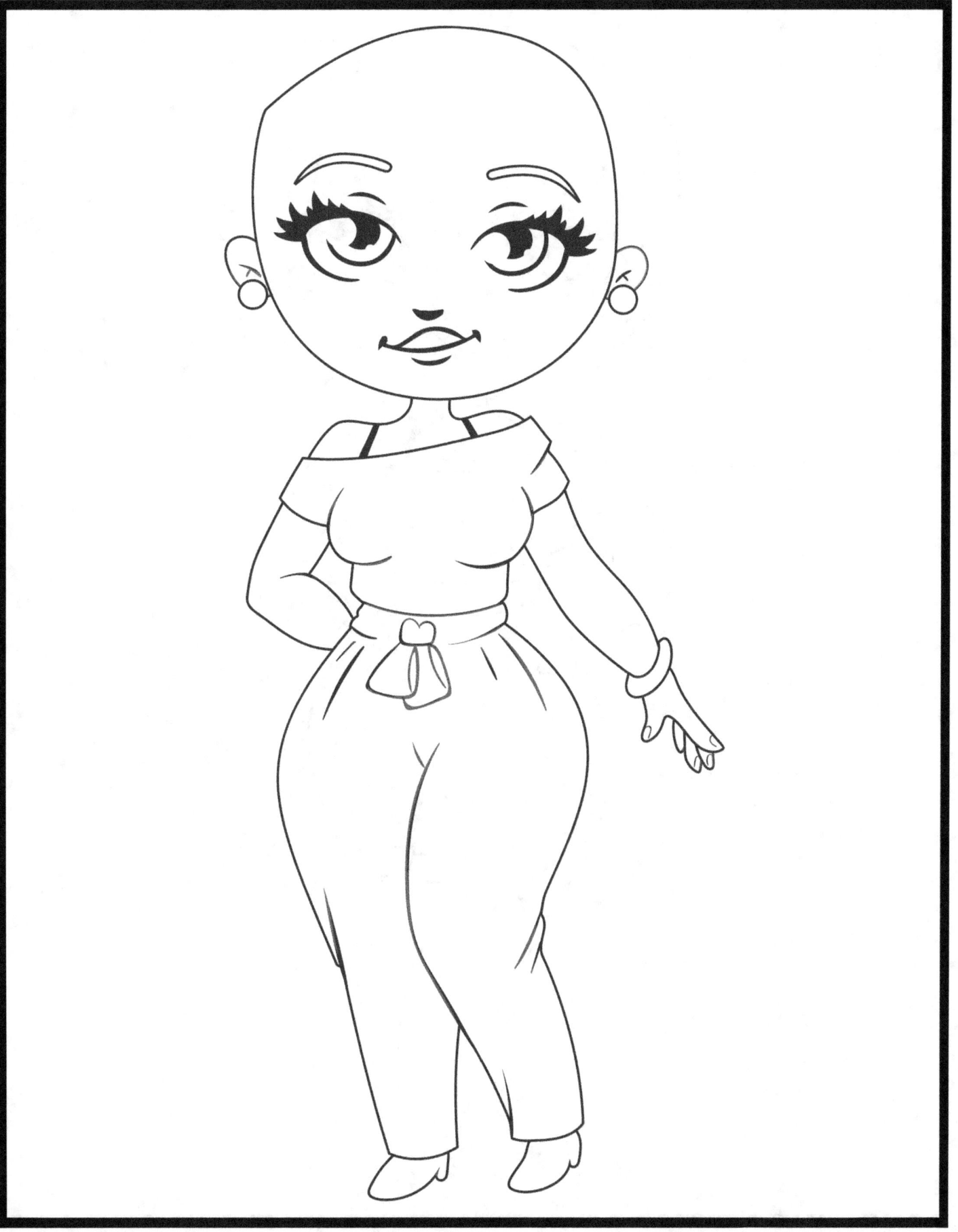

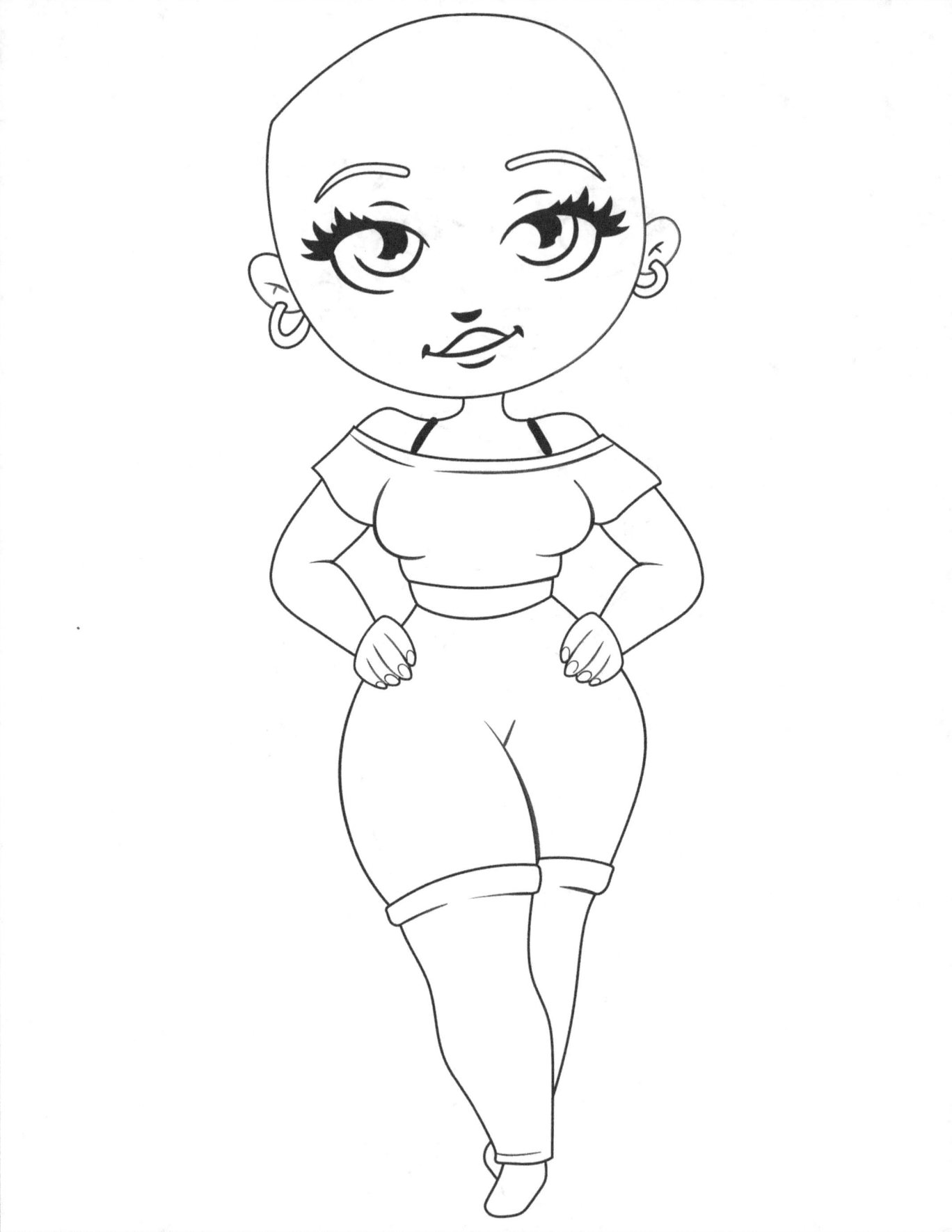

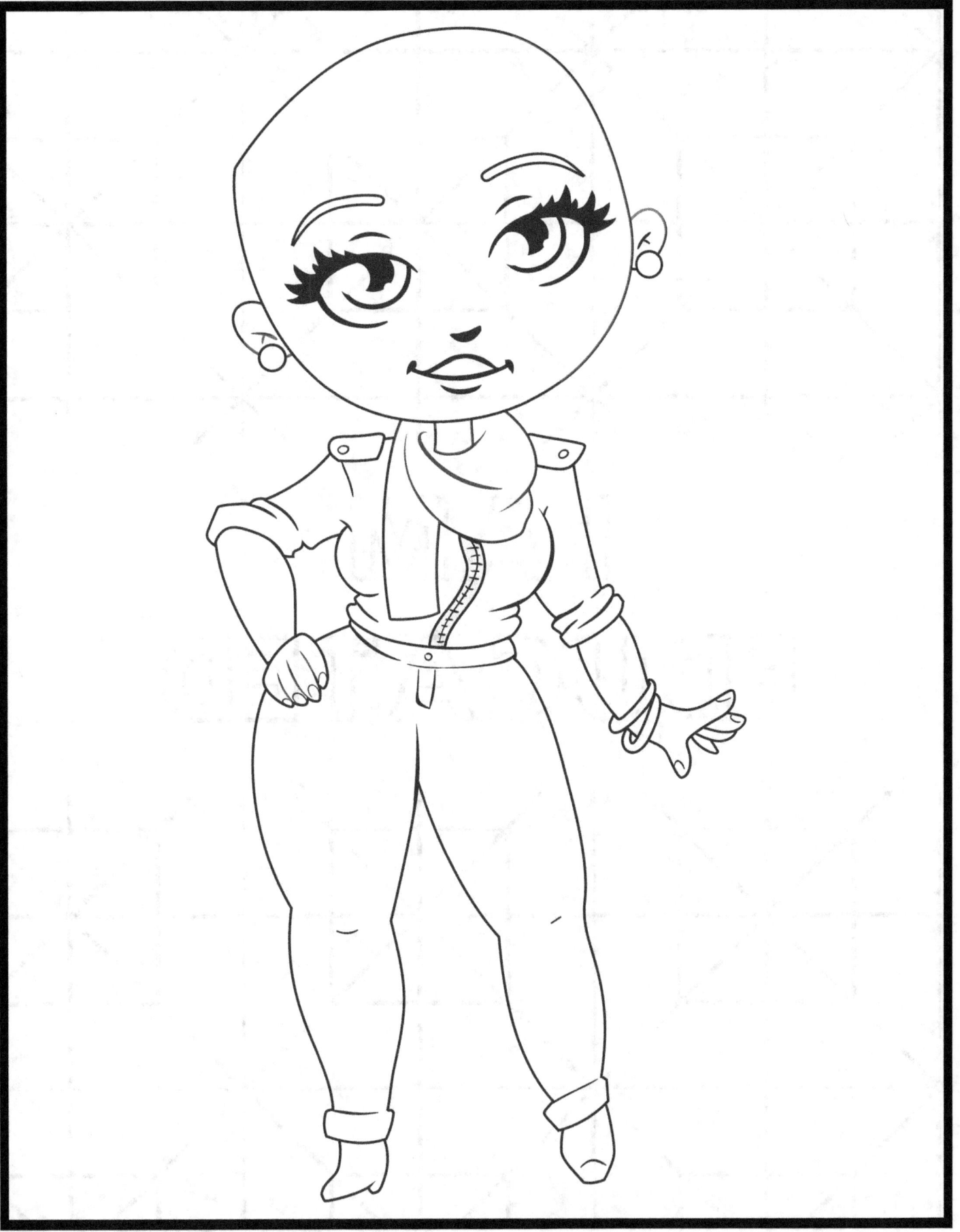

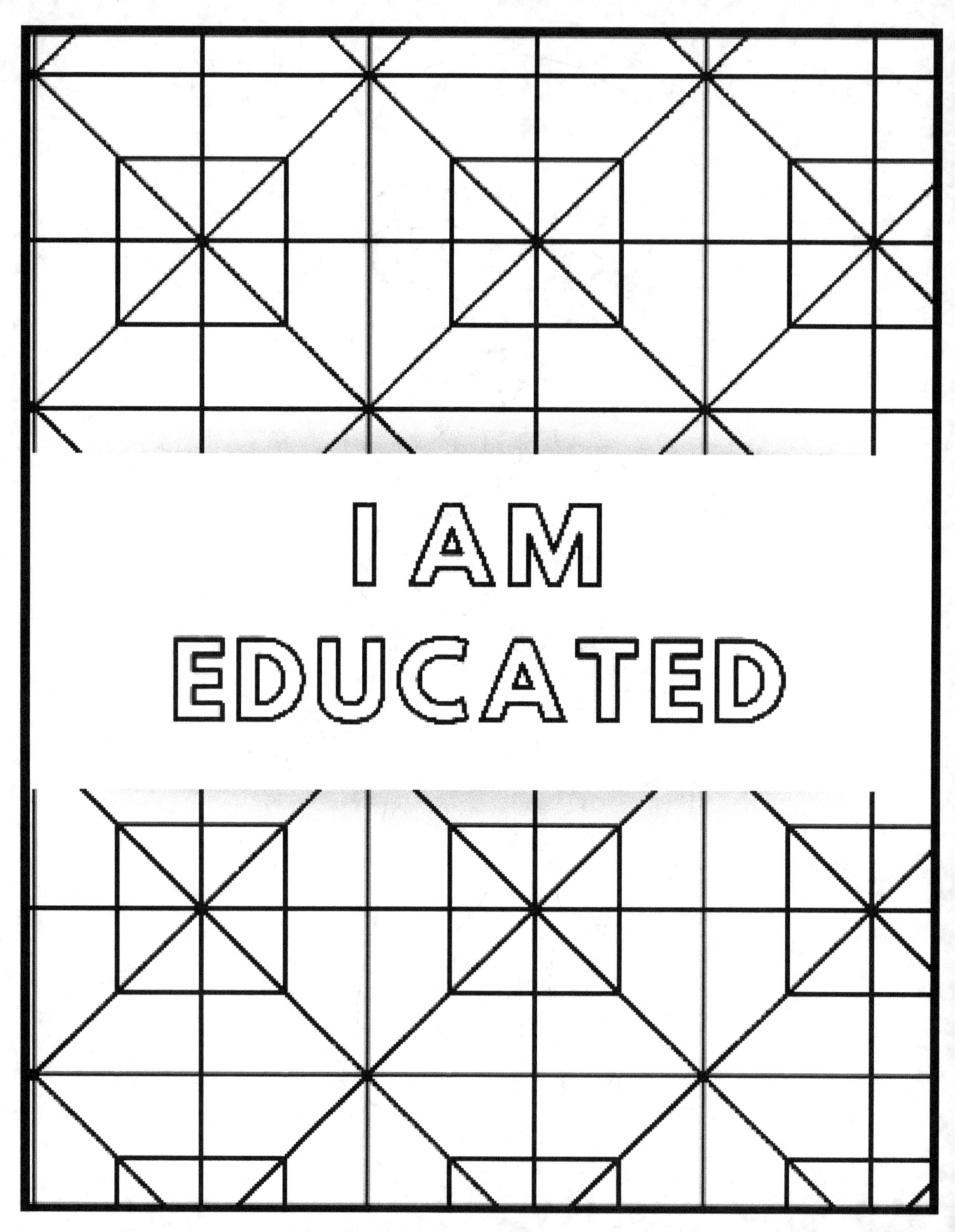

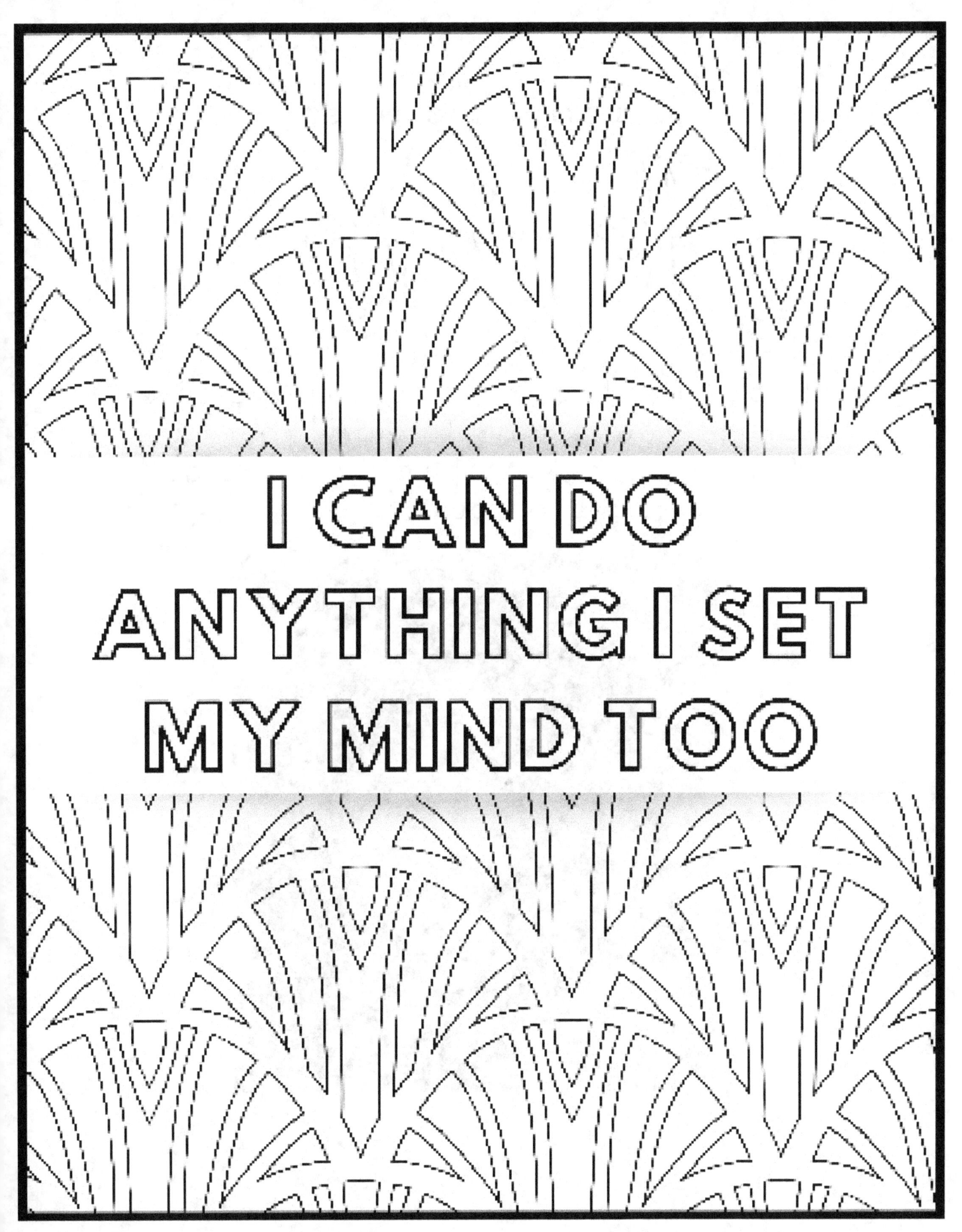

a warm note to say

Thank You!

Queen,
I Hope This Book Inspired, Empowered & Uplifted You In Ways To Make Your Mind, Spirit & Creativity Shine. Never Forget Who Your Are!

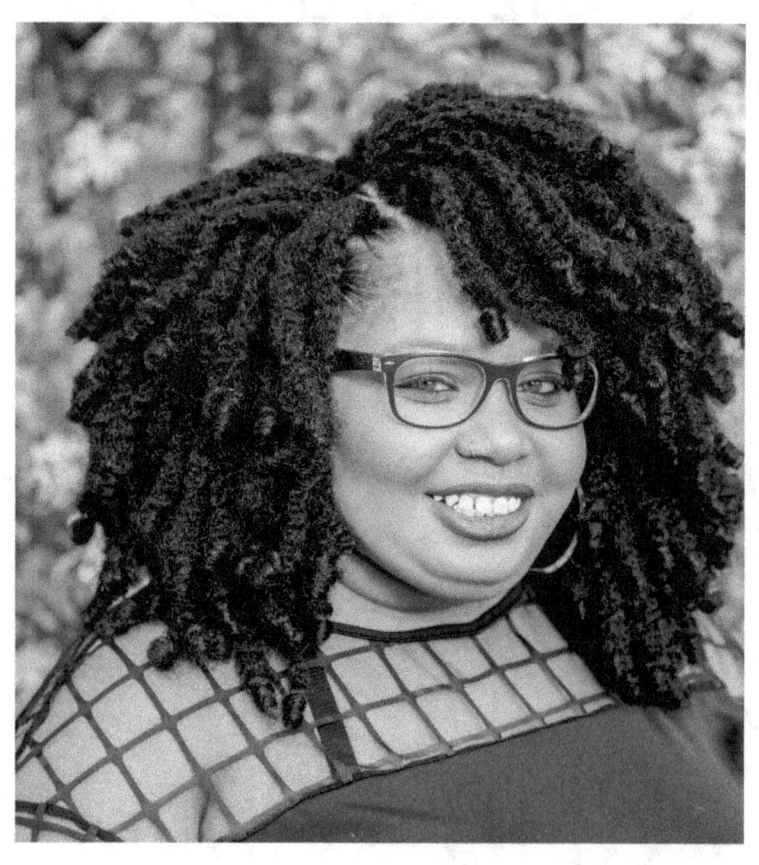

Malika O'Neill

www.ingramcontent.com/pod-product-compliance
Lightning Source LLC
Chambersburg PA
CBHW080520220526
45465CB00006B/2543